The Wonders of Emotional Intelligence for Teens & Young Adults

8 Powerful Tools to Improve Your People Skills, Gain Personal Insights, Grow Social Awareness, and Crush Everyday Stress

by Pearl Fagan

Copyright © 2025 B3H Consulting, Writing, & Publishing; Author: Pearl Fagan

The content within this book may not be reproduced, duplicated, or transmitted without direct written permission from the author or the publisher.

Under no circumstances will any blame or legal responsibility be held against the publisher, or author, for any damages, reparation, or monetary loss due to the information contained within this book, either directly or indirectly.

Legal Notice:
This book is copyright protected. It is only for personal use. You cannot amend, distribute, sell, use, quote, or paraphrase any part of the content within this book, without the consent of the author or publisher.

Disclaimer Notice:
Please note the information contained within this document is for educational and entertainment purposes only. All effort has been expended to present accurate, up-to-date, reliable, and complete information. No warranties of any kind are declared or implied. Readers acknowledge that the author is not engaged in the rendering of legal, financial, medical, or professional advice. The content within this book has been derived from various sources.
Please consult a licensed professional before attempting any techniques outlined in this book.

By reading this document, the reader agrees that under no circumstances is the author responsible for any losses, direct or indirect, that are incurred as a result of the use of the information contained within this document, including, but not limited to, errors, omissions, or inaccuracies.

Contents

INTRODUCTION	7
CHAPTER 1: KNOWING YOUR FEELS IN AN EMOTIONAL WORLD	9
CHAPTER 2: SELF-AWARENESS > GET TO KNOW YOUR REAL SELF	17
CHAPTER 3: SELF-CONFIDENCE > EMBRACING YOU	29
CHAPTER 4: SELF-REGULATION > KEEPING YOUR COOL	43
CHAPTER 5: EMPATHY > WALKING IN SOMEONE ELSE'S SHOES	53
CHAPTER 6: SOCIAL SKILLS > VIBING WITH OTHERS	65
CHAPTER 7: COMMUNICATION > MAKING YOUR VOICE HEARD	77
CHAPTER 8: MOTIVATION > FUELING YOUR INNER DRIVE	93
CHAPTER 9: NAVIGATING CHANGE > THRIVING IN TRANSITIONS	105
CHAPTER 10: BUILDING STRONG RELATIONSHIPS	121
CHAPTER 11: EMOTIONAL INTELLIGENCE IN THE DIGITAL AGE	139
CHAPTER 12: LIFE SKILLS FOR THE REAL WORLD	149
CHAPTER 13: THRIVING AND GROWING	167
CONCLUSION	183
THOUGHT SPARKS & TECHNIQUES	185
GLOSSARY OF EMOTIONS	225
REFERENCES	229
ABOUT THE AUTHOR	235
BOOKS IN THE WONDERS OF HOLISTIC WELLNESS SERIES	237
BOOKS FROM THE PUBLISHER	241

INTRODUCTION

You know that feeling when you are about to present in front of the whole class, and your hands get all sweaty? Or when you and your best friend have a fight and it feels like the end of the world? Yeah, we have all been there. Being a teen and even a young adult is like being on a wild roller coaster in the dark! There are ups, downs, and a bunch of loop- de-loops, half of which you cannot see until you are halfway into it. It is a lot to handle, right?

This is where this book comes in: here to help you level up your emotional game! The goal is to build your emotional intelligence (EI) skills, also known as emotional quotient (EQ). These skills are amazing tools that can make a huge difference in your life. They can help you understand yourself better, connect with others on a more meaningful level, and make smarter choices all around.

So, what exactly is emotional intelligence? Well, it is sorta like having a superpower... It helps you understand your own feelings as well as those of others. It is about knowing how to keep your cool when things get heated, about being able to bounce back when life throws a curveball, and about making friends... and keeping them. EQ is a big deal, especially during these years when you are in the midst of figuring out who *you* are.

Learning to manage your emotions can boost your confidence and help you build stronger relationships. It can even improve your grades because you are better at handling stress. Picture this: you are facing a big test, and instead of freaking out, you take a deep breath and focus. That is EQ in action.

Let me tell you a bit about myself. I am Pearl, an experienced corporate trainer in emotional intelligence, and I have seen first-hand how these skills transform workplaces.

I am also a long-time practitioner of mindfulness meditation and a proud mom of two teenagers and one young adult. Watching them navigate their own emotional ups and downs has inspired me to bring EQ to young people just like you. And I truly believe that if we can learn these skills early on, our life journeys can be so much smoother.

Now, you may be asking yourself, 'What makes this book different?' Or maybe you might think, "Self-help books are boring!" or "They never work!"

I totally get it! But please, give this one a shot! It is fun, engaging, and easy to apply. It is designed for you, the reader, to actually use in your daily life. It is packed with interactive exercises and journaling prompts, which I prefer to call Thought Sparks! I have even included stories from different cultures to make them relatable to everyone. I use simple language and a practical approach. This is not a textbook. It is more like having a chat with a close friend who gets what you and what you are going through.

This book is broken down into easy-to-navigate chapters. We start by understanding emotions. Then, we move on to building resilience and tackling social dynamics. There are also interactive tools along the way to keep things interesting. It is not just about reading; it is about doing, reflecting, and growing.

I encourage you to dive into the exercises and thought sparks, as practice is key to developing your EQ. Think of this book as a hands-on guide to becoming the best version of yourself.

So, are you ready for this journey of self-discovery? Embrace it! By the end, you will be better equipped to handle whatever life throws your way. You will be more confident, resilient, and ready to shine.

Let us get started and see where this adventure takes us!

CHAPTER 1: KNOWING YOUR FEELS IN AN EMOTIONAL WORLD

"Emotions can be as unpredictable as the weather."

You know when you are at the school dance, and suddenly your crush walks in? Your heart races, your palms sweat, and you cannot remember how to act cool. Or maybe you are in class, and the teacher calls on you when you are totally unprepared. Instant panic, right? These moments are part of being a teen and young adult, where emotions sometimes feel like they are calling the shots. But what if you had a secret weapon to handle all these feels? That is where emotional intelligence, or EQ, steps in. It is like having an inner guide to help you understand and manage emotions, yours, and others. Whether you are facing peer pressure, a friendship fallout, or just a bad day, EQ can help you navigate through life's twists and turns.

Emotional Intelligence Vs. Book Smarts

Now, let us talk about EQ versus IQ. You have probably heard about IQ, which is the number people use to measure how "smart" someone is, right? It focuses on solving math problems, understanding language, and figuring out puzzles. It is great for school stuff, like acing that math test or writing an essay. But Here is the deal: life is not just about numbers and facts. It is about people, emotions, and relationships, too. That is where EQ comes in. EQ is all about understanding your emotions, knowing what you are feeling and why. It is about dealing with those emotions in a healthy way. It is also about empathy, which means understanding how others feel and responding in a caring way. So, while

IQ helps you solve a tricky math problem, EQ helps you handle a tough conversation with a friend.

Do not get me wrong, EQ and IQ are not enemies! They are more like teammates. You need both to succeed. Think about group projects. You will use IQ to research and come up with ideas. But you will need EQ to work well with others, share ideas without arguing, and listen to your teammates. Or imagine studying for a big exam. Your IQ helps you understand the material. Your EQ helps you manage stress so you do not burn out. Both types of intelligence work together to get things done.

Meet Jamie, for example, a high school student. Jamie is super smart and always gets top grades. But Jamie struggles with friends. One day, their friend Alex gets upset because Jamie keeps interrupting during conversations. Instead of arguing, Jamie decides to use EQ skills. They listened to Alex and apologized for interrupting them. Jamie now realizes that understanding and respecting Alex's feelings is important. Thanks to EQ, Jamie learns to be more empathetic, and this strengthens their friendship. This example shows that while IQ can get you far in academics, EQ is what helps you build meaningful relationships.

Some people think EQ is not as important as IQ. They believe that being book-smart is the key to all success. But that is simply not true. Sure, IQ can help you get good grades or solve problems. But EQ is just as crucial, maybe even more, for real-life success. It helps you deal with stress, communicate better, and build strong relationships. Studies show that people with high EQ often succeed in their careers and have satisfying personal lives. So, do not underestimate the power of EQ. It can help you thrive in ways IQ alone cannot.

So, why should YOU care about EQ? Because it is a skill that you can learn and improve upon! You can practice being more aware of your feelings and how you react. You can learn to listen to others and understand their feelings. These skills make life smoother. They help you deal with challenges, like a tough teacher/boss or a fight with a friend. And the best part? You can get better with practice.

Just like you practice sports or music, you can practice EQ. You will notice your relationships improving, stress decreasing, and confidence growing.

EQ really is a game-changer. It is all about getting to know your feels and handling them like a pro.

Salty Or Sweet? How To Name Your Emotions & Take Control

Let us imagine emotions as a playlist. You have got your happy tunes, your sad ballads, the angry rock songs, and everything in between. But sometimes, you hit shuffle, and it feels like every emotion is playing at once. So, how do you sort through this chaotic playlist? The first step is naming your emotions. It might sound simple, but giving a name to what you are feeling can change everything. When you say, "I feel anxious," instead of just feeling off, you take control. You start to understand what is happening inside. Naming your emotions helps you see them clearly. It is like turning on a light in a dark room. Suddenly, that overwhelming feeling is not so scary. You can handle it. You can decide what to do next.

Being able to name your emotions is not just about feeling better yourself. It also helps you connect with others. Imagine trying to solve a puzzle without knowing what the pieces look like. That is what it is like trying to understand someone else's feelings without understanding your own. When you know your emotions, you can see others' feelings more clearly. You can put yourself in their shoes. This is empathy. It is like a super tool that helps you build better friendships and connections. And your emotional vocabulary is a big part of this. The more words you know to describe your feelings, the better you can express them. When you express your emotions clearly, others can understand you better, too.

But how do you build this emotional vocabulary? Start by learning new words to express your feelings. Make a list of emotions and what they mean. Read books that talk about different feelings. Notice words that describe how characters feel. Try using these words in your conversations.

You might even keep a feelings journal, where you write down what you feel each day and why. Over time, you will find yourself better at talking about emotions. You might say, "I feel overwhelmed," instead of just, "I am stressed." This practice helps you and those around you understand each other better.

Sometimes, emotions can be close but not the same. Like how "frustrated" and "angry" feel similar but are not identical. Learning to spot these differences can help you manage your emotions better. Try exercises that make you think about similar emotions. What makes "nervous" different from "excited"? Practicing this can help you react more calmly when emotions hit. You can say, "I am nervous," instead of letting that feeling control you.

To really get the hang of this, practice expressing emotions. Role-playing can be fun for this. Pretend you are in different situations and think about how you would feel. Act it out. It helps to express feelings out loud. You can also use creative outlets like writing poems or stories about emotions. Or draw and paint how you feel. These activities help you explore your emotions deeply and express them in unique ways.

When you expand your emotional vocabulary, you boost your emotional intelligence. It is like learning a new language. The more words you know, the better you can communicate. With a richer vocabulary, you understand your feelings more. You can manage them better. You become more aware of how others feel, too. This makes you a better friend and helps you in all kinds of situations. You may find that you are less worried about what others think. You might also feel more confident speaking up in groups because you can express yourself clearly.

Let us try a practical exercise. Start an emotion diary. Write down what you feel each day. Name the emotions. Use new words you have learned.

Reflect on why you felt that way. This practice helps you spot patterns. You might notice you feel anxious before tests or happy after seeing friends.

Over time, you will see how this helps you understand and control your emotions better. It is a simple step, but it can make a big difference.

From Vibes To Drivers: Navigating Your Emotional Landscape And Understanding Emotional Drivers

Picture your emotions like the weather. Some days, it is all sunshine and rainbows. On other days, it feels like a storm is brewing inside you. Just like how the weather changes from sunny to cloudy, your emotions can shift from happy to sad or from calm to anxious. This ever-changing mix of feelings is what we call your emotional landscape. It is the backdrop of your feelings and moods. And just like with the weather, understanding the patterns of your emotions can help you prepare and respond better to life's ups and downs, even the unexpected ones.

Now, let us talk about emotional drivers. These are the hidden forces that steer your emotional vehicle. They are the reasons behind how you react to different situations. Think of them like the fuel that powers your emotional engine. Sometimes, it is easy to see what drives your feelings. Maybe you are upset because you had a bad day, or you are excited because you got some good feedback. But other times, these drivers are buried deep. They might come from past experiences or things you do not even realize affect you.

Emotions can be as unpredictable as the weather. One moment, you are floating on a cloud of happiness, and the next, you are caught in a downpour of frustration. It is important to recognize how these fluctuations impact your daily life. By mapping out your emotional landscape, you can gain self-awareness. Try to keep tabs on your emotions throughout the day. Notice what triggers certain feelings and how long they last. This practice helps you spot patterns. Maybe you realize that you always feel anxious before lunch because you are worried about an afternoon test. Once you know that, you can work on calming down before the test.

Understanding your emotional weather means identifying both strong and subtle feelings. Some emotions are loud, like anger or excitement. While others are quiet, like the slight unease you feel when something is off. It is crucial to notice these subtler emotions. They can be clues to what is really going on inside. Often, emotions show up in your body. Your heart might race when you are nervous, or your stomach might flutter with excitement. Learning to connect these physical sensations with your emotions can help you understand yourself even better.

Again, behind every emotion, there is a driver. Sometimes, these drivers are emotional themselves. They come from your feelings and experiences.

Maybe you feel jealous because you have been left out in the past. Other times, drivers are rational. They come from your thoughts and logic. For example, you feel worried about not having enough time to study because you know you have a big test. These drivers can shape how you respond to situations. Understanding them can help you see why you react the way you do.

Let us explore some common emotional drivers. Fear can make you avoid situations that seem risky. Joy might push you to chase after fun experiences. Anger can drive you to stand up for yourself when you feel wronged. By digging deeper into your emotions, you can uncover these drivers. Ask yourself why you reacted a certain way. What were you feeling beneath the surface? Understanding these motivations can help you make more informed choices.

Your emotions and their drivers play a big role in decision-making. Imagine you are deciding whether to join the school play. You feel excited because you love acting, but you are also scared of messing up. Your emotional drivers, like excitement and fear, will influence your choice. Knowing this, you can use your drivers to your advantage. Set goals that align with what drives you emotionally. If excitement about acting is a strong driver, focus on that when you are scared. Channel your energy into positive directions that match your emotions.

As you navigate through life, remember that understanding your emotional landscape is key. It helps you see the bigger picture and make better choices. Recognizing your emotions and what drives them gives you power over how you react. You learn to respond with intention rather than just reacting impulsively. This awareness becomes a superpower that helps you thrive in different situations. So, embrace your emotions, the sunny and the stormy ones. They are an essential part of you, guiding you through the adventure of life.

CHAPTER 2: SELF-AWARENESS > GET TO KNOW YOUR REAL SELF

"You are your own kind of awesome!"

Imagine you are at a party. Everyone is dancing, and you feel out of place, like you are the only one wearing a costume at a casual hangout. You start thinking, "Should I change to fit in?" This feeling is super common. It is the fear of standing out. But Here is the twist: standing out is your secret superpower. This chapter is all about finding your unique vibe and loving it. Your individuality is what makes you, well, you. It is the quirky laugh, the love for obscure bands, or even the way you see the world. Embracing these traits is key. It is about knowing what makes you different and owning it.

Standing out can feel scary. What if people do not get you? What if they think you are weird? Take a deep breath. You are in good company. Think of stars like Ed Sheeran or Taylor Swift. They did not fit the mold. Ed was the kid with glasses and a guitar, while Taylor wrote songs that told her truth. Their uniqueness became their strength. They turned what made them different into their shining light. You can do that, too. It is about finding what makes you tick and letting it shine. You do not have to be like everyone else.

You are your own kind of awesome!

Building confidence in your individuality takes practice. Start with small steps. Try telling yourself positive affirmations each day. Things like, "I am enough," or "My uniqueness is my strength." These words might feel cheesy at first, but over time, they will build your confidence.

Set boundaries, too. It is okay to say no to things that do not feel right for you. It is okay to stand up for what you believe in. These actions help you stay true to yourself. They remind you that your voice matters. You do not have to change to fit in. The right people will love you for who you are.

Being true to yourself has big benefits. It can make your relationships better. When you are authentic, you are more likely to attract people who appreciate the real you. It is like a magnet. Genuine self-expression can lead to deeper connections. Take Olly Alexander from Years & Years, for example. He uses his platform to encourage others to be proud of their identity. His authenticity strengthens his bond with fans. You can experience this, too. When you embrace who you are, you find happiness. You let go of trying to be someone you are not. You feel more connected to the world around you.

Thought Spark: Find Your Unique Vibe

Take a moment to write down three things that make you unique.
Are you the one who always knows the best memes?
Do you have a knack for making people laugh?
List them out.

Then, think about why these traits are special.
How do they make you feel? How do they impact your life?

Reflect on how you can embrace these traits even more.
Try sharing them with friends or using them in a new project.

Embrace what makes you different, and let that light guide you!

Mirror, Mirror: Understanding Your Emotional Triggers

Ever felt like you are on top of the world, and then someone says something, and boom—your mood crashes? That is the magic of emotional triggers. They sneak up on us, causing intense feelings out of nowhere. It could be a small comment that feels like criticism or a joke that hits a sore spot. Maybe it is a moment when you trip in front of everyone, and embarrassment floods in. These situations can trigger strong emotions, sometimes without warning. Recognizing these triggers is the first step. Think about what sets you off. Is it when someone questions your abilities? Or when you feel left out? Knowing your triggers helps you prepare for them.

Now, let us dig a bit deeper. Why do these triggers affect us so much? Many emotional triggers trace back to past experiences or beliefs. Maybe you grew up hearing that you had to be perfect. Or there was a time when you felt rejected, and that feeling stuck with you. Childhood experiences shape how we react today. If you were teased as a kid, criticism might sting more now. Understanding these roots helps us handle them better. It is like pulling weeds from a garden. You need to get to the root to stop them from growing back. By tracing back to where these feelings started, we can begin to change how we react in the now.

Being self-aware of these triggers is like having a map of that emotional landscape of yours. Start by noticing the lead-up to a trigger. What happens right before you get upset? Is it a certain word or situation? Try creating a mental checklist for these moments. When you feel your heart racing or your face heating up, take a step back. Breathe. Ask yourself, "What just happened?" This process helps you understand what sets you off and gives you a chance to react differently. It is not about avoiding these situations entirely. It is about knowing how to handle them when they appear.

Mindfulness can be a game-changer here. It is about staying present and being aware of your emotions without judgment. Notice the physical sensations that come with your feelings. When you feel anger, your fists might clench. When you are nervous, your stomach might do flips.

Recognizing these sensations can help you pause and choose how to respond. Mindfulness acts like a pause button. Instead of reacting right away, you take a moment to breathe and think. It helps you manage your emotions better and keeps you from saying or doing something you might regret later.

So, the next time you feel a strong emotion coming on, remember this: pause, breathe, and reflect. Recognize the trigger, understand its roots, and choose your response. You have the power to change how you react.

Shadow Work: Facing Your Emotional Blind Spots

Have you ever wondered why certain things bug you so much or why you react a certain way? It is like having a shadow that follows you around, but you cannot quite see it. This is what we call shadow work. It is all about exploring those hidden parts of yourself—the stuff you do not always notice or want to face. Imagine your mind as a room. Shadow Work is like turning on a light in the darkened corners. When you shine a light on these areas, you start to understand yourself better. This idea comes from the study of psychology. It is like peeling back layers to find what is underneath. Carl Jung, a famous psychologist, introduced this concept. He believed that by understanding our shadow, we can become more whole. It is not about being perfect. It is about being real and honest with ourselves.

To start shadow work, you need to spot your emotional blind spots. These are the feelings and behaviors you do not always see. Maybe you get angry when someone interrupts you, but you do not know why it bothers you so much. Or perhaps you shy away from new challenges because you are afraid of failing. These are your blind spots. One way to find them is by asking for feedback. Talk to a friend or someone you trust. They might see things you do not. Like when your best friend says, "Hey, you always seem upset when we talk about school." This can be a clue to what is hiding in your shadow.

Why bother with shadow work? Well, simply put, it is because it helps you grow. It is like finding a hidden treasure. When you face your blind spots, you improve yourself. You get to know who you really are. This can make your relationships better. You are more empathetic because you understand your own feelings and struggles. And when you get to know your shadow, you become more patient with others. It is like a ripple effect. You change, and it affects everything around you. There are stories of people who have done shadow work and transformed their lives.

They became more understanding, less judgmental, and more open to new experiences.

How do you do shadow work? There are lots of ways. Guided exercises can help. Close your eyes and think of a situation that bothers you. What do you feel? Where is it coming from? You can also try therapy or counseling.

These are safe spaces where you can explore your emotions with a professional as they help guide you through the process. Shadow Work is not a quick fix. It is something you do over time. It is like a workout for your mind; the more you practice, the stronger your self-awareness becomes.

Finding Your Values: What Really Matters To You

Think of life as a road trip. Without a map or GPS, it is easy to get lost or end up where you never wanted to go. Personal values are like that GPS, guiding you through choices and decisions. But what are they, really?

Values are the things that matter most to you. They are the core beliefs that drive your actions and decisions. They shape your life, even when you do not realize it. Sometimes, these values come from family or culture. Other times, you develop them on your own. It is important to sort out what is truly yours from what you have inherited. Your values serve as your inner compass, helping you navigate through the ups and downs.

Finding your values is like figuring out what makes your heart sing. It might feel tricky at first, but it is worth the effort. Try this: think about moments when you felt truly happy or proud. What were you doing? Who were you with? Those moments often reflect your core values. You can also do a value sorting exercise. Write down a list of different values like honesty, adventure, kindness, or success. Then, rank them by importance.

Which ones feel essential to you? Another way is to visualize your ideal life. Picture a day where everything feels right. What are you doing? Who is around you? These images can help you uncover what matters most.

Living by your values means making choices that align with them. Let us say one of your values is creativity. If you are deciding between a science or art class, you might lean towards art. It might be more fulfilling for you. Or, if you value honesty, you might choose to speak up even when it is hard.

Real-life decisions often involve weighing your values against each other. Maybe you value both friendship and honesty, but a friend asks you to keep a secret you are not comfortable with. It might mean having a tough conversation to stay true to yourself. These decisions are not always easy, but they help you live authentically.

Values also play a big role in relationships. Shared values can bring people closer. For example, if you and your friend both value adventure, you might plan exciting trips together, but differing values can cause friction. If one friend values punctuality while the other is more laid-back, it might lead to misunderstandings. It is important to recognize and communicate these differences. Understanding each other's values can strengthen bonds. It helps you respect each other's perspectives, even if they are not the same.

Values are like a special glue that holds relationships together or, sometimes, the sandpaper that causes friction. Recognizing this can help you navigate friendships and family dynamics more smoothly. It is all about understanding what matters to you and respecting what matters to others.

Mastering Mindfulness: Staying Present With Emotions

Imagine standing in a busy hallway with people rushing past you. It is loud, and there is a lot going on. Now, picture yourself pausing for a moment.

You take a deep breath, and suddenly, the chaos seems to fade a bit. This is what mindfulness feels like. It is about being right here, right now. Mindfulness means paying attention to the present moment without getting caught up in worries about the past or future. It helps you connect with what is happening inside and around you. It is a tool that can make a big difference in how you handle emotions. When you are mindful, you notice your feelings without letting them take over. This can help you feel calmer and more in control.

Practicing mindfulness can be super simple. Start with mindful breathing. You do not need anything fancy. Just focus on your breath. Inhale through your nose, hold it for a moment, then exhale slowly through your mouth. Do this a few times. Notice how it makes you feel. It is like giving your mind a mini vacation. Another technique is the body scan. Close your eyes, and slowly focus on each part of your body from head to toe. Notice any tension, and try to let it go. This helps you become aware of how your emotions affect your body. Then, there is mindful eating. Next time you eat, really taste your food. Notice the flavors and textures. Eating becomes an experience rather than just a routine.

Mindfulness plays a big role in understanding your emotions. Being present helps you see what you are feeling and why. Instead of reacting impulsively, you pause and think. It gives you space to choose how to respond. For example, when you feel angry, mindfulness helps you recognize the anger without letting it explode. You might remember the story of a student who practiced mindfulness before exams. By focusing on their breathing, they felt less anxious and more focused. Mindfulness practitioners often share how this practice enhances emotional awareness. They notice their reactions and understand them better. This awareness can help you improve relationships and handle challenges with more ease.

Living a mindful life does not mean sitting in silence all day. It is about weaving mindfulness into daily activities. You can practice mindful walking by paying attention to each step. Notice how your feet feel on the ground.

Listen to the sounds around you. Or try mindfulness during chores, like washing dishes. Feel the water, notice the bubbles, and be fully there in the moment. These small practices can add up to a big change. They help you stay balanced and centered even when life gets hectic. Mindfulness is a mental workout, and the more you practice, the stronger your emotional awareness becomes. It is a skill that benefits you in all areas of life.

Taking time for mindfulness can change how you see the world and yourself. It helps you pause and breathe, even in stressful times. As you move forward, keep this practice in mind. It will continue to support you as you explore more about yourself and your emotions. Next, we will explore how to handle self-doubt and build confidence in who you are.

△△△

CHAPTER 3: SELF-CONFIDENCE > EMBRACING YOU

"Speaking up is powerful. It shows the world who you are and what you stand for!"

Imagine waking up to a world where everyone likes your latest post. Your phone buzzes with heart emojis, and your friends are all talking about it. It feels good, right? But then, what if the next day, those likes disappear? Suddenly, you start to question yourself. This is the tricky dance we all have with the need for validation. It is like chasing shadows, always slipping through your fingers. When you rely on others to feel good about yourself, your confidence becomes fragile as it no longer belongs to you.

You are always waiting for approval, whether it is on social media or in real life. It feels like you are riding a rollercoaster, with extreme ups and downs depending on what others say or think about you.

Social media can be a double-edged sword; on the one hand, it connects you to friends and trends. On the other, it can make you feel like you are never enough. You see perfect images and wonder why your life does not look the same. But Here is the secret: those images are not always real. They are curated highlights, often with filters and editing. When you chase likes and comments, you are seeking external validation. It is temporary and depends on others. You cannot control it. But there is another way. Internal validation is about finding approval within yourself. It is relying on your own feelings and judgments. It is more stable and long-lasting.

Thirsty For Validation? Finding Confidence Within

To build internal confidence, start with self-reflection. Take a moment to think about what makes you proud. What do you like about yourself? Write it down. Reflecting helps you see your strengths and what matters to you. It shifts your focus from others to yourself. Inner dialogue is another tool. Pay attention to how you talk to yourself. Are you your own worst critic? Try changing that narrative. Instead of saying, "I messed up," say, "I can learn from this." Your words have power. Use them to lift yourself up, not tear yourself down. This practice improves your inner dialogue and boosts self-assurance.

Self-reliance is key to confidence. It is about trusting your abilities and making decisions for yourself. Start by setting small goals and working towards them. Achieving these goals builds trust in your own capabilities, and you will realize that you can handle challenges. This independence enhances personal growth and self-esteem. It shows you that you do not need others to define your worth. You have got this. Your achievements, big or small, are your own. Celebrate them. They are proof of your strength and resilience.

Self-affirmations are a great way to reinforce internal validation. Try a daily check-in with yourself. Each morning, look in the mirror and say something positive. It might feel awkward, like talking to a stranger. Stick with it. Say things like, "I am enough," or "I am capable." Keep it simple and genuine. These affirmations remind you of your worth. They become a habit and slowly change how you see yourself. They help you build a foundation of confidence that does not depend on others. It is like planting seeds of self-love and watching them grow. You are nurturing your self-confidence from the inside out.

Thought Spark: Finding Confidence Within

Take a few minutes each day to write down three positive things about yourself.

They can be simple, like "I am kind" or "I am creative." Repeat them out loud.

Notice how they make you feel.

This exercise will help you focus on your strengths and grow your confidence.

Snatched: Celebrating Your Achievements

Think about the last time you accomplished something, even if it seemed small. Maybe you finished reading a book, scored a goal, or aced a test. Did you take a moment to celebrate? Recognizing achievements, no matter how tiny, is crucial. It boosts your self-worth and gives you that extra motivation to tackle the next challenge. You see, celebrating your wins is like giving yourself a high-five. It tells you, "Hey, I did this, and it is awesome!" Whether it is a small victory or a major milestone, acknowledging it only reinforces belief in your own abilities. It is a reminder that you are capable and that your hard work pays off!

Keeping track of your accomplishments can help you see your progress more clearly. One way to do this is through achievement journaling. Write down what you achieved today, this week, or this month. It does not have to be grand. It could be as simple as finishing an assignment on time or helping a friend. Over time, you will have an actual record of all the amazing things you have done. Another fun idea is to create a visual achievement board. Use photos, clippings, or drawings that represent your successes. Hang it somewhere that you will see often. It is like a constant reminder of your growth, what you have accomplished, and that you have the ability to keep going.

Gratitude plays a big role in celebrating success. When you appreciate what you have achieved, you start to value your efforts more. Try gratitude exercises that focus on your accomplishments. At the end of the day, think of three things you are proud of and grateful for. This habit helps you see the positive side of things. It teaches you to appreciate not just the big wins but also the small steps you take every day. Gratitude turns your attention to what you have done well rather than what you have yet to get done.

Also, sharing your successes with others can build a supportive community around you. Let your friends and family know about your achievements. It could be a simple text, a phone call, or a post on social media. But remember, it is not about bragging. It is about sharing joy and inviting others to celebrate with you. When using social media, keep it positive and genuine. Focus on the experience rather than just the result. If you prefer real-life connections, consider hosting mini celebrations. Invite loved ones over for a casual get-together to mark your accomplishments. Sharing your joy strengthens your bonds with those who care about you. They become your cheerleaders, and you become theirs!

Flexing Your Strengths: Recognizing What You Are Good At

Have you ever thought about what makes you stand out? We all have strengths, like hidden gems waiting to be discovered. Finding them is like a treasure hunt. Start by looking back at your achievements. What have you done that made you proud? Maybe you nailed a special project, crafted a great piece of art, or helped a friend through a tough time. Reflecting on these moments can show you what you are naturally good at. Another way is to ask others for feedback. Talk to friends, family, or teachers who know you well. They might see strengths you have not noticed. Sometimes, we need others to help us see the full picture of ourselves.

Once you know your strengths, it is time to use them in everyday life. Have you got a knack for organizing? Use it to plan your next big projects. Break tasks down, make lists, and set deadlines. You will find things get done more smoothly. If you are creative, like drawing or coming up with ideas, try using it to solve problems. When faced with a challenge, think outside the box. Your creativity can be your secret weapon. Strengths are like tools in a toolbox, and the more you use them, the better you get. They make tasks feel lighter and more enjoyable.

It is also important to see the value in diverse strengths. Everyone has got different talents. That is what makes teamwork powerful. When working in a group, look at what each person brings to the table. Maybe one friend is great at research, while another excels at speaking. Use these strengths to assign roles. This way, everyone shines, and the group does better.

Celebrating these differences helps everyone feel valued. It is like being part of a band. Each instrument adds to the harmony. Together, you create something amazing. Recognize and appreciate these different strengths, and you will find teamwork more rewarding.

Let me tell you about Alan, a student who discovered a talent for leadership. Alan always enjoyed organizing events for the school club but felt unsure about leading. One day, the teacher asked Alan to head up a project. At first, Alan hesitated, worried about making mistakes. But with encouragement, they took the leap. Through trial and error, Alan found a knack for bringing people together and guiding them toward a common goal. The club event was a success, and Alan's confidence soared. This experience taught them that sometimes our strengths reveal themselves when we actually take a step outside of our comfort zone.

Body Confidence: Feeling Good In Your Skin

Have you ever stood in front of a mirror and just sighed? You are not alone. Many teens and young adults face body image issues. Society often tells us how we should look. Magazines show perfect models. Social media is full of edited photos. It is a lot of pressure. Everyone seems to have flawless skin and perfect hair. But Here is the truth: those images are not always real. They are polished, filtered, and full of AI creations. Nobody wakes up looking like that. Unrealistic beauty standards can make you feel less confident. They make you *think* you are not good enough. But remember, <u>everyone is unique</u>. Your body is yours, and it is amazing just the way it is.

So, let us talk about some ways to feel better about your body. Start by practicing gratitude for what your body can do. You may be a great runner, or you can dance like nobody's business. Focus on those abilities. They are more important than any picture-perfect look. Try writing down things that you appreciate about your body. It could be anything, like being able to laugh with friends or hug someone you love. Also, consider engaging in activities that promote physical well-being. Exercise is not just for looking a certain way. It is about feeling good and having fun. Whether it is playing sports, going for a walk, or dancing in your room, find something that makes you happy.

Being savvy about all types of media is important, too. When you see ads or posts, look closely. Ask yourself if those images are realistic. Challenge the portrayals that seem too on-point, and remember that they are designed to sell products, not to show real life. So now, every time you see an ad, think about what it is trying to make you feel and what it is actually trying to sell. Then remind yourself that it is just marketing. Doing this can help you separate what you see from how you feel about yourself.

Take John, a teen who struggled with their body image. They felt pressure to look a certain way, just like everyone else. But things changed when Jamie joined a basketball team. Playing and practicing the game made John feel stronger and more confident. Their focus shifted from looks to what their body could achieve. John realized that feeling good was not about fitting into a certain expectation; it was about celebrating what their body could do and how it felt. This new perspective brought empowerment and happiness to John, and they fully embraced their body's unique qualities and ultimately felt more confident every day!

Speaking Up: Making Your Voice Heard

Imagine you are in a group discussion, and you have an idea buzzing in your mind. You want to share it, but something holds you back. Speaking up can feel intimidating, like shouting into a void where everyone is listening. Yet, speaking up is powerful; it shows the world who you are and what you stand for. When you express your needs and opinions clearly, you take control of *your* narrative. You advocate for yourself, whether it is in a classroom or work setting, with friends, or at home. Assertive communication is your tool. It helps you share your thoughts and stand your ground without being aggressive or passive. It is about finding your voice and using it with confidence.

To communicate effectively, you need more than just words. Your body language speaks volumes. Stand tall, make eye contact, and use gestures to emphasize your points. A confident posture can make a big difference. It shows you are engaged and ready to contribute. Crafting concise messages also matters. Think about what you want to say before you say it. Keep it clear and impactful. This way, your message will not get lost in the chatter.

Mastery comes with effort. It is like learning to play an instrument. The more you practice, the more natural it feels, and it will become easier to speak up and be heard.

To many, public speaking might sound scary, but it is a great way to build confidence. Look for opportunities to hone this, such as joining a debate club or taking part in a public speaking workshop. These settings provide a safe space to work on your skills. If that is not your thing, try presenting something in front of friends or family. They can give you feedback and support. Practicing in a comfortable environment helps you find your rhythm. It prepares you for bigger stages. You will learn to control your nerves and communicate with clarity. Public speaking is not just for politicians or actors. It is a skill that everyone can benefit from!

Take Mia, for example; she wanted to make a difference in her community and had noticed a lack of recycling programs at her school. Instead of staying silent, Mia decided to organize a project to raise awareness about recycling. With clear communication and passion, she rallied students and teachers to support her vision. Her project not only improved the school's recycling efforts but also inspired others to take action. Mia's story shows how speaking up can lead to real change. It highlights the impact of assertive communication and the courage to stand up for what you believe in. You might even find new friends who share the same passion!

Handling Criticism: Use It, Do Not Lose It

Criticism can often feel like a punch to the gut, especially when it comes across as harsh or unfair. But not all criticism is meant to hurt. Understanding the difference between constructive and destructive criticism is key. Constructive criticism is like a coach guiding you to improve. It is meant to help you grow by pointing out areas where you can do better. Destructive criticism, on the other hand, is often just negative noise, not aimed at helping. Recognizing feedback aimed at improvement is the first step. If someone offers a suggestion on how to improve your essay or performance, that is constructive. It can be a valuable tool for growth.

When someone criticizes you, it is natural to feel defensive. But try to separate your emotions from the feedback. Take a deep breath and focus on the words being said, not how they make you feel. This helps you process the information more clearly. If the critique is unclear, do not hesitate to ask for clarification. Say something like, "Can you give me an example of what you mean?" This shows you are open to understanding and improving.

Remember, criticism is not an attack on who you are. It is just a chance to learn something new. By staying calm and open, you turn criticism into a chance for growth.

Adopting a growth mindset towards criticism can change how you see it. Instead of viewing criticism as a setback, see it as an opportunity to learn. Reflect on the feedback and identify areas for improvement. Ask yourself what you can do differently next time. This kind of reflection helps you see criticism as a stepping stone to success. It is like adjusting your course after hitting a bump in the road. You learn, adapt, and move forward. This mindset makes you more resilient and open to feedback, no matter how tough it seems.

Let me tell you about Sam, a student who struggled with criticism in art class. Sam loved drawing but often felt crushed by critiques. Instead of giving up, Sam decided to embrace the feedback. Sam worked on the areas pointed out and practiced tirelessly. Over time, Sam's skills improved significantly. Sam learned to see criticism not as a roadblock but as a way to get better. This change in attitude led to bigger opportunities and greater confidence. Sam's story shows how criticism, when used wisely, can be a powerful catalyst for personal growth. It can push you to reach new heights you never thought possible.

As you think about handling criticism, remember it is part of learning and growing. Next, we will dive into the art of keeping your cool under pressure. Get ready to explore ways to stay calm and collected, even when life gets chaotic.

CHAPTER 4: SELF-REGULATION > KEEPING YOUR COOL

"Let your anger fuel your art or music; turning fire into art!"

Imagine that you are about to enter an intense video game tournament. Your heart's racing, your palms are sweaty, and that little voice in your head is screaming, "Do not mess up!" Sound familiar? It is easy to get lost in the chaos of emotions, especially when the stakes feel high. But what if you could hit pause on that inner chaos and find your calm? That is where a peaceful mindset comes in.

A peaceful mindset is like having a calm lake inside you, where your thoughts and emotions can chill. It helps you stay cool, even when life tries to stir things up. But cultivating this inner peace is not about ignoring emotions; instead, it is about being the boss of them. With practice, you can learn to ride the waves of stress and anxiety without getting swept away. And you get to enjoy moments more fully without that looming sense of chaos.

So, how do you create this serene mental state? Let us start with visualization. Think of a place that makes you feel relaxed. It could be a beach, a forest, or even your cozy bedroom. Close your eyes and imagine yourself there. What do you see? What do you hear? Let your mind wander through this peaceful scene. Visualization is a powerful tool. It can transport you to a calmer state of mind whenever stress strikes.

Another way to foster tranquility is through sparks of gratitude. Each day, write down two to three things that you are grateful for. They do not have to be big; it could be a good laugh with a friend or your favorite song playing on the radio! Gratitude shifts your focus from what is wrong to what is right. It helps you see the silver lining, even on tough days. Over time, this practice can build a more positive outlook. It can make your mind feel lighter and more at peace with less effort.

Progressive muscle relaxation (or body scan meditation) is another technique to try. It involves tensing and then relaxing different muscle groups in your body. Start from your toes and work your way up to your head. As you relax each muscle, imagine the tension melting away. This exercise can help you feel more grounded and less anxious. It is like hitting the reset button for your body and mind. It is also a great technique for falling asleep!

Your surroundings also play a big role in your mindset. A cluttered space can make your mind feel cluttered. Try decluttering and organizing your room. Create a personal sanctuary filled with things that bring you joy and calm. It could be soft lighting, calming scents, or your favorite posters. A peaceful environment can help you feel more centered and focused.

Mindfulness is key to maintaining this peaceful mindset. It is about staying present and aware of your thoughts and feelings. Practice daily mindfulness routines, like mindful breathing or walking. You can even try mindful eating, where you savor each bite and focus on the flavors. These practices help you connect with the present moment and find calm amidst the chaos.

Crush Your Self-Control: Pause, Breathe, Reflect

Say you are in a heated chat, and your fingers are ready to send that message you will regret later. We have all been there. But what if you could hit pause first? Pausing gives you the power to think before you act. It is like having a secret weapon against impulsive reactions. Counting to ten is a classic move. Those ten seconds can make all the difference. They give your brain a chance to catch up with your emotions. It is like stepping back from the edge just in time. Walking away is another strategy. When things get tense, take a break, move to a different room, or go for a short walk. Distance can give you a fresh perspective, and you will find that problems often look smaller when you are not right up against them.

Breathing is your best friend when it comes to calming down. Simple breathing exercises can work wonders. Try the 4-7-8 technique. Inhale through your nose for four counts, hold for seven, and exhale slowly through your mouth for eight. It is like a mini-reset for your mind and body. Or try box breathing. Inhale, hold, exhale, and hold again. Each for four counts. This method can bring immediate stress relief. Breathing deeply helps slow your heart rate and clear your mind. It is like pushing a giant reset button inside of you. You do not need special tools or lots of time; just a few minutes and some focus.

Reflecting on your actions helps build self-control. After a stressful event, take some time to think about it. Write down your thoughts in a journal.

What happened? How did you react? What could you do differently next time? This practice helps you learn from your experiences. Keep in mind that this reflection is not about beating yourself up; it is about understanding your reactions and finding ways to improve. When you look back and see how you have handled things, you can spot patterns. You may notice you always get upset about the same stuff.

Recognizing these patterns lets you change them or better manage them in these moments of unrest.

Take Tiffany, for example. She was always stressed about exams. She started using these reflection techniques. After each test, she wrote down what worked and what did not. Over time, she found better study habits and stress management methods. Her grades improved, and so did her confidence. Tiffany's story shows how reflection can lead to real change. It is not about being perfect. It is about making progress. By pausing, breathing, and reflecting, you can gain control over your actions. You learn to respond thoughtfully instead of reacting impulsively. This control can lead to better decisions and happier outcomes.

When To Hit Pause: Managing Emotional Outbursts

Say you are sitting in class when your teacher hands back a test, and your grade is not what you expected. You feel the heat rising in your face. Your fists clench under the desk. Ever felt that way? Emotional outbursts can catch you off guard, especially when stress from school or work piles up. Maybe you had a rough day with friends, and you are tired, then someone says the wrong thing. Boom, you explode. Recognizing what sets you off is a game-changer. Start by thinking about moments when you lost your cool. Was it a snarky comment from a friend or a bad mark on a quiz? When you know your triggers, you can brace yourself and respond differently.

Calming down during a meltdown is not easy, and it definitely takes practice. Grounding techniques can help you stay rooted in the present. Try the 3-3-3 method: look around and name three things you see; focus on three sounds you hear; and finally, identify smell three scents around you. Doing this shifts your mind from chaos to calm, pulling you away from the storm and into a safe harbor. It may feel weird at first, but with time, it becomes second nature. Your mind stops racing, and you can think clearly again. It makes you feel like you have more control over your emotions.

High emotions can make it tricky to talk. But you can still communicate effectively. Start with "I" statements. Instead of saying, "You always make me mad," try, "I feel upset when..." It helps you own your feelings without blaming others. If things get too heated, take a break. Step out for a bit. This is not running away. It is giving yourself space to cool down. Sometimes, just five minutes can make a huge difference. You return with a clearer head. Conversations are more productive when everyone is calm. It reduces the chance of saying something you will regret later.

Quick Stress Busters: Fixing Your Overwhelm

Trying to juggle homework, a part-time job, and social plans is like trying to balance a stack of plates on a unicycle. And that stress can hit you out of nowhere, especially when you have academic or work deadlines breathing down your neck. Pressure from school can feel like a mountain on your shoulders. And then, there is the social side—friends, family, and the unspoken rules of fitting in. It can be overwhelming, and you might feel like you are expected to be everywhere all at once. These demands can pile up, making you feel like you are drowning in expectations. But do not worry; there are ways to keep your head above water.

In those high-pressure moments, quick stress relief can be your lifesaver. Let us start with deep breathing. It is simple, and you can do it anywhere. Take a slow, deep breath through your nose. Hold it for a few seconds, then let it out slowly through your mouth. Feel your shoulders relax with each exhale. This practice helps calm your mind and body. Visualization is another tool you can use. Close your eyes and picture a place that makes you feel calm. It might be a beach, a forest, or anywhere you feel peaceful. Let your mind wander there for a few moments. These techniques can help you find your center when things get chaotic. Many will even combine the two: close your eyes, imagine a peaceful place, and then breathe deeply in, hold for a few seconds, and exhale.

Physical activity is another great stress-buster. Moving your body releases endorphins, which are like little happiness boosters. You do not need a gym membership or fancy equipment. Simple workouts at home can do the trick. Try a quick session of jumping jacks, yoga, or even a quick, 30-second dance party in your room! The goal is to get your blood pumping and your mind off stress. Exercise not only helps reduce stress, but it also improves your mood and energy levels. It is like giving yourself a mini-vacation from worries.

Handling Anger: Cool Down Without Blowing Up

We have all been there. You are playing a game, and suddenly, a friend crosses a line. Maybe they tease you about something personal, or you feel like they are not being fair. Your insides start to boil. Anger is like that. It sneaks up when boundaries are crossed or when things seem unfair. It is important to know what sets you off. Recall those moments when someone did not respect your space or when a teacher seemed to favor another student. Recognizing these triggers can help you see them coming and prepare. You do not have to let anger control you. You can learn to handle it before it handles you and ultimately takes over.

When anger starts bubbling up, you need to act *before* it explodes. One trick is slowly counting to ten. It sounds simple, but those ten seconds can give your brain a moment to cool off. It helps you pause and think. Another way is to channel that energy into something creative. Grab a sketchbook or pick up a guitar. Let your anger fuel your art or music. It is like turning fire into art. You get to express yourself, and it feels good. Plus, it distracts you from the anger and gives you a chance to cool down. You end up with something beautiful rather than a regretful outburst.

Anger itself is not bad; it is how you handle it that really matters. Learning to express it in a healthy way is key. This is where constructive communication comes in. Use "I" statements to share how you feel. Instead of saying, "You never listen..." try saying, "I feel unheard when..." This approach focuses on your feelings rather than blaming others. It opens up a space for real conversation without making the other person defensive.

Setting boundaries is also important. Let others know what you need to feel respected. You might say, "I need some space when I am upset," or "Please do not interrupt when I am speaking." Clear and respectful boundaries help prevent triggers.

Take Sarah, for example, a teen who used to struggle with anger. Whenever her siblings teased her, she would lash out, which only made things worse.

One day, she decided to try something different. Instead of yelling, she took a deep breath and counted to ten. Then, she calmly told her siblings how she felt using "I" statements. To her surprise, they listened and stopped teasing. Sarah also started painting when she felt angry, creating beautiful art pieces from her emotions. Her relationships at home improved, and she felt more in control. Sarah's story shows that with the right tools, you can turn anger into a powerful force for good.

Anxiety Hacks: Staying Calm In The Chaos

Have you ever felt your heart pounding like a drum before a big presentation or when walking into a crowded room? Well, that is anxiety, tapping you on the shoulder. It is your body's way of saying, "Get ready!" This feeling is called the fight-or-flight response. It is like your brain's alarm system, designed to protect you. But sometimes, it kicks in when

there is no real danger, just simple nerves. Social situations can be big anxiety triggers. Meeting new people or speaking in front of a group can make your palms sweat and your mind race. It is like your body is on high alert, even when everything is actually fine.

But do not worry; there are ways to calm that chaos. One method is the progressive muscle relaxation technique that I previously discussed. By tensing and releasing each muscle group, starting from your toes and moving up, your body lets go of tension. Visualization can also be a

lifesaver. Picture yourself conquering that anxiety-inducing scenario with confidence. See yourself speaking smoothly or walking into a room with a smile. These techniques can shift your focus and calm your nerves.

Creating a personal anxiety toolkit can make a huge difference. Think of it as a collection of things that bring you comfort and peace. It could be a playlist that makes you smile, a stress ball, or a favorite book. Breathing exercises specific to your needs should be included, too. Practice different techniques discussed throughout this book and find what works best for you. Having this toolkit ready means you can reach for it whenever anxiety creeps in. It is your secret weapon to staying calm.

Let us learn from Julia, a student who struggled with anxiety before giving presentations.

She felt like her heart was about to leap out of her chest. So, she created a toolkit with her favorite music, a small notebook for doodling, and a few deep breathing exercises. Before each presentation, she would take a few minutes to listen to a song, draw something silly, and breathe deeply. It helped her calm down and focus. Over time, she grew more confident and less anxious about speaking in public. Julia's story shows how having a plan and the right tools can help you handle anxiety more effectively.

Understanding anxiety and having strategies to manage it can transform how you face challenges. By using the right tools and techniques, you can stay calm and in control. This chapter has equipped you with the skills to keep your cool and manage anxiety. Next, we will explore how empathy and understanding can improve your relationships and help you connect with others on a deeper level.

CHAPTER 5: EMPATHY > WALKING IN SOMEONE ELSE'S SHOES

"Compromise isn't about losing. It's about collaborating to find a solution that works for everyone."

Imagine you are in the lunchroom, and you see your friend sitting alone, poking their food. You think, "Should I go over?" This is where empathy comes in. It is like having a radar that senses what others are feeling. When you walk in someone else's shoes, you get a glimpse of their world. You understand their feelings and thoughts. It is like being a superhero whose power is kindness. Empathy helps you connect with others on a deeper level. It is the keystone to building strong friendships and communities. When you show empathy, you create a safe space where people feel heard and valued. It is like saying, "I am here for you, no matter what."

Showing Up For Your Squad: Building Emotional Support Networks

Having a supportive group around you is like having a safety net. Emotional support networks are groups of friends or family who stand by you. They help you navigate life's ups and downs. These networks enhance your emotional well-being. They give you a sense of belonging and security.

When you have people who understand you, it feels like you can conquer anything. A strong support network is full of cheerleaders who celebrate your wins and lift you up when you are down.

It is a place where you can be yourself without fear of judgment.

Building your support network starts with identifying the people who make you feel good. These are the friends and family members who listen and care. Look for those who share your interests and values. They could be classmates, teammates, or even neighbors. Once you have found them, work on strengthening those bonds. Spend quality time together. Share your thoughts and listen to theirs. Trust grows when you open up and show vulnerability. It is like watering a plant. The more you nurture it, the stronger it becomes.

Being a supportive friend is just as important as having one. It is about being there for others when *they* need you. Offer a listening ear and a shoulder to lean on. Practice active listening. Focusing on what your friend is truly saying without interrupting or thinking about how you are going to respond shows that you care. Sometimes, just being present can be enough. You do not always need to solve their problems. Simply listening can make a world of difference. Ask and offer help without judgment. Let them know you are there, no matter what. Empathetic support is a gift you can give anyone.

Empathy is the foundation of any strong support network. It strengthens connections and builds trust. When you empathize with others, you see the world through their eyes. It helps you understand their struggles and joys.

Empathy bridges gaps and fosters understanding. It reminds us that we are all human, with feelings and dreams. It is a powerful tool that brings people together. When you practice empathy, you create a ripple effect. Your kindness inspires others to do the same. Together, you build a community where everyone feels valued and loved. Empathy is not just a skill; it is a way of living. It is about making the world a little brighter, one connection at a time.

What Is The Tea? Listening To Understand, Not Just Reply

Say you are at lunch, and your friend is telling you about their day. You nod, but your mind drifts to your phone or what you will say next. We have all been there. But Here is the catch: true listening means more than hearing words. It is about understanding the whole story. It means focusing fully on the speaker and showing them you care. Eye contact is key. It tells your friend, "I am here, and I am listening." But try not to stare too hard, though, as it might get a bit awkward! A simple nod or saying "I see" goes a long way in making them feel heard. These small actions show you are engaged. You are not just waiting for your turn to talk.

But what gets in the way? Sometimes, it is the buzzing phone that steals your attention. Those notifications can wait. Put your phone face down or on silent. Give your friend the space they deserve. Then there are the judgments we might not even notice. Maybe you think you already know what your friend will say, so you tune out. Or you assume their story is not important. Challenge these thoughts. Keep an open mind. Everyone's story is worth hearing. By setting aside judgments, you open the door to real understanding. It is like clearing the fog to see the road ahead.

When you listen with intent, magic happens. You build stronger bonds. Your friend feels valued. They know they can trust you. Take Audrey and Jack, for example. They were close but had drifted apart. One day, Audrey decided to really listen to Jack's worries. She did not interrupt. She just listened. This simple act brought them closer than ever. They worked through their issues and rebuilt their friendship. Active listening turned a rocky path into a stronger connection. It can resolve conflicts, too. By listening, you understand where the other person is coming from. You find common ground and work things out.

Want to practice? Try a listening exercise. Pair up with a friend. One person shares a story, and the other listens without interrupting. Then switch. Focus on what the other person says. Notice their expressions and tone. Afterward, share what you heard. It is a simple exercise, but it strengthens your listening skills. You will notice how much more connected you feel to your friend. These skills are like muscles. The more you use them, the stronger they get. Soon, listening will come naturally. You will be the friend everyone wants to share their stories with.

The Art Of Asking Questions: Getting To The Heart Of The Matter

Have you ever been in a conversation that felt like a game of ping-pong? You say something, they say something, and it goes back and forth, but it never really goes anywhere. That is where asking the right questions can change everything. Think of questions as keys that unlock the door to deeper understanding. When you ask open-ended questions, you invite the other person to share more. Instead of asking, "Did you like the movie?" try, "What did you think about the movie?" This simple change encourages the other person to open up. It gives them space to share their thoughts rather than just a yes or no.

Reflective questions are another powerful tool. They prompt deeper thinking and can shift the conversation to a more meaningful place. You might ask, "How did that situation make you feel?" or "What did you learn from that experience?" These questions show that you care about the other person's perspective. They help you see the world through their eyes. When you dig a little deeper, you build a stronger connection. It is like finding hidden treasure in a conversation. You uncover insights and emotions that might otherwise stay buried.

Different types of questions can shape a conversation in various ways. Leading questions, for example, can nudge someone to a specific answer. They might sound like, "Do not you think that idea is great?" These can limit openness and make the other person feel boxed in. Clarifying questions, on the other hand, aim to clear up confusion; something more like, "Can you explain what you mean by that?" They invite the speaker to expand and clarify their thoughts. Knowing when and how to use these questions can enrich your dialogue. It makes conversations more engaging and thoughtful.

Sometimes, just asking, "What do you need right now?" can be a game-changer. It is simple yet full of empathy. It shows you are there to support, not just to talk. Another empathetic question might be, "What has been on your mind lately?" These questions open doors, encouraging the other person to share what they are comfortable with. They let you step into their world for a moment. When you show genuine curiosity, you create a safe space for others to be themselves.

Cultivating a mindset of curiosity and openness in conversations is like opening a window to fresh air. It means being genuinely interested in what the other person has to say. It is about embracing the unknown and being okay with not having all the answers. When you encounter unfamiliar situations, approach them with curiosity. Ask questions that explore new ideas and perspectives. This openness not only enriches your understanding but also deepens your relationships. It allows you to connect with people on a level that goes beyond the surface.

Respectful Interactions: Meeting People Halfway

Think about the last time you had a disagreement with someone. It could have been over something small, like which movie to watch, or something bigger, like a group project. How did it feel? When we interact with others, respect should be our starting point. It is about treating others how they want to be treated, which is usually quite similar to how you would want to be treated. Respectful interactions mean listening when someone speaks and speaking kindly, even if you disagree. You know that warm feeling when someone genuinely listens to you? That is respect in action. On the flip side, disrespect can sting, like when someone interrupts you or dismisses your ideas. It can make you feel small, as if your voice does not matter to anyone. So, how do we make sure respect is at the heart of all our interactions?

First, let us talk about fostering respect. <u>It starts with active listening</u>, really hearing what the other person is saying without planning your next response while they talk. Acknowledge their viewpoint, even if you do not agree. Use language that shows you care about their perspective. Say things like, "I see your point," or "That is interesting." Keep your tone calm and steady. Avoid raising your voice, even if the conversation gets heated. When you show respect through your words and actions, you create a space where everyone feels safe to express themselves. It is like building a bridge between you and that other person.

Compromise is another key player in respectful interactions. It is about finding a middle ground where both sides feel heard and valued. Imagine you are deciding on a group project topic. You want one thing, and your friend wants another. Instead of digging in your heels, consider options that incorporate both ideas. Negotiation techniques can help. Suggest, "How about we combine our ideas?" or "What if we tried your idea this time and mine next time?" These tactics show that you are willing to meet halfway.

Compromise is not about losing. It is about collaborating to find a solution that works for everyone. It strengthens respect and builds trust.

Take a moment to think about your interaction style. How do you usually communicate with others? Are you the type to speak up, or do you hang back and listen? Self-assessment can be eye-opening. Try asking yourself questions like, "Do I listen more or talk more?" or "Do I give others space to share their thoughts?" You can also ask friends for feedback. They might see things you do not. Friends can offer insights into your habits, like if you tend to interrupt or if you always take charge. Use this information to adjust and improve how you interact. When you reflect on your style, you become more aware of how your actions affect others. This awareness helps you grow and build more respectful relationships.

Ghosting And Its Consequences: Respectful Communication

Now, let us talk about ghosting. It is when someone disappears from a conversation or your life without a trace. One moment, you are chatting, and the next, they are gone - no explanations, no replies, and no goodbye. Ghosting happens in friendships, dating, and even with family. You might send a text and never hear back. It is like talking into a void, and it can

leave you feeling confused and hurt. It makes you wonder what went wrong. Ghosting can be a tough pill to swallow. It can affect your mental and emotional health. You start doubting yourself and feel rejected. It is as if someone slammed a door in your face, and you never saw it coming.

The emotional impact of ghosting can be intense. It might make you question your self-worth. You might feel angry, frustrated, or sad. The lack of closure can haunt you. You might replay conversations in your head, trying to figure out where things went wrong. It is like a puzzle missing its final piece. These feelings are normal, but they can be heavy. They can linger and affect how you see yourself and others. Ghosting can create a cycle of doubt and insecurity. It leaves you feeling like you are in limbo, unsure of what to do next.

Tap into your empathy, and instead of ghosting, consider using direct communication. It is a way to handle relationships with respect. If you need to end a friendship or relationship, be honest. It does not mean you have to have a long conversation. A simple message can suffice. Let the person know how you feel and why you need space, using those 'I' statements as a helpful tool. This might feel awkward, but it is kinder in the long run. It gives both of you closure. Granted, they might not like what you have to say, but they will appreciate the honesty. Direct communication is about being clear *and* kind. It is about respecting the other person's feelings in the matter.

Setting boundaries is also important. Let people know what you need in a relationship. You may need more space or less texting. Be upfront about it. Clear boundaries help prevent misunderstandings. They show others how you want to be treated. They protect your emotional energy. Keep in mind, though, that boundaries are not walls. They are simply guidelines that make interactions healthier. When you set boundaries, you are taking care of yourself and respecting others.

Empathy is key in all communication. Consider how your actions affect others. Put yourself in their shoes. Think about how you'd feel if roles were reversed. Empathy-driven communication means you prioritize kindness and understanding. It is about being mindful of others' feelings. When you communicate with empathy, you build stronger connections. You create a space where everyone feels heard and respected. Empathy makes conversations more meaningful, even the tough ones.

As we wrap up this chapter, remember that empathy and respectful communication can transform relationships. They help you handle tricky situations with care. Next, we will explore how to navigate social dynamics and build connections that last.

Unlock the Power of Emotional Intelligence

"Teens equipped with emotional intelligence today become the confident, resilient leaders of tomorrow." -Pearl Fagan

Dear Reader,

Emotional intelligence is not just a skill; it's a game-changer. It empowers teens and young adults to connect, grow, and thrive; even in life's most overwhelming moments.

My mission with *The Wonders of Emotional Intelligence for Teens & Young Adults* is to equip young people with the tools they need to navigate emotions, build meaningful relationships, and handle stress with grace. But to reach more readers, I need your help!

Your feedback can make a huge impact. Sharing your thoughts about my book not only helps others discover these transformative tools, but it also inspires more teens to unlock their emotional superpowers!

Simply scan the QR code below to leave your review! It only takes a few minutes, and your words could make a lasting difference for countless teens.

Thank you for your support. Your review means the world to me and to every young person who will benefit from these insights.

Warmest regards,

Pearl Fagan

Scan me

CHAPTER 6: SOCIAL SKILLS > VIBING WITH OTHERS

"The more you express yourself, the more creative and confident you become"

Say you are at a concert, music thumping, lights flashing, and all around you are people dancing and singing along. You might know a few faces, but mostly, you are surrounded by strangers. Yet somehow, in that moment, you feel connected. It is like everyone is part of one big, happy squad. Building your own squad in everyday life can feel just as electric and fulfilling. Having a social circle is more than just having people to hang out with. It is about having a crew that supports you, lifts you up, and makes life a little bit brighter.

A supportive social circle is like a personal cheer squad; they are there when you need emotional support. Maybe you are feeling down about a rough day at school or work. They are the ones who listen and offer comfort. They are also your motivators, encouraging you to chase your dreams and reach your goals. They remind you that you can do anything, even when you doubt yourself. Having people who believe in you can make all the difference.

They help you see the possibilities, even when you cannot see them for yourself. That is the magic of a strong social circle.

Building Your Squad: Finding Your People

Finding your people might seem daunting, but it is easier than you think. Start by looking for places where you can meet like-minded individuals. Join clubs or organizations that match your interests. Love art? Find an art club. Into sports? Check out a team. These groups are full of people who share your passions. They make it easy to connect and form friendships.

Participating in community events or activities is another great way. Attend local fairs, workshops, or exhibitions. These gatherings provide a chance to mingle and meet new folks.

When forming friendships, remember to keep an open mind. Be inclusive and welcome different perspectives and backgrounds. Everyone has a story to tell, and you might learn something new. It is like adding different colors to a painting. Each shade makes the picture more vibrant and interesting.

Embracing diversity enriches your life and broadens your understanding of the world. It helps you grow and develop empathy. Be open to the unexpected; sometimes, the best friendships come from the most unlikely of places.

Let me share a story. Meet Emma and Zoe, two teens who lived in the same neighborhood but never really talked. They both joined a local gardening club to help out with a community project. At first, they were just friendly strangers, working side by side. But as they planted and pruned together, they discovered a shared love for gardening and a knack for silly jokes. Over time, their friendship blossomed much like the flowers they tended. They supported each other through thick and thin, proving that shared hobbies can lead to strong bonds. Emma and Zoe's story shows that friendships can bloom when you least expect it.

Flexing Without Stressing: Balancing Self- Expression And Humility

Expressing yourself is like splashing colors on a blank canvas. It is how you show the world who you are. When you let your creativity flow, you boost your confidence. You discover parts of yourself that you did not know were there. You may find a love for painting, writing, or music, but you must be willing to try new things to find it. These outlets give you a way to release your thoughts and feelings. They let your true self shine. Creating something unique can make you feel proud and powerful. It is like saying, "This is me, and I am awesome!" The more you express yourself, the more creative and confident you become.

But Here is the twist: self-expression needs a buddy called humility. Think of humility as the quiet friend who keeps you grounded, whispering in your ear. It reminds you that while your voice is important, so are others' voices. Humility fosters mutual respect and understanding. It means recognizing that everyone has something valuable to share. It is about listening to others and learning from them. Imagine you are in a group project, and everyone wants their idea to shine. A little humility helps you see the big picture. It is about finding a balance. You can express yourself without overshadowing others. This balance creates harmony, where everyone's voice gets heard.

Balancing self-expression with humility is not as hard as it sounds. Start by listening and sharing equally. When you are in a conversation, make sure to hear others out. Give them the same attention you want for yourself. Try not to interrupt or dominate the discussion. It is like a dance, where everyone gets a turn in the spotlight. Acknowledge others' contributions, too. If a friend suggests a great idea, give them credit. Say, "I love your idea!" This simple act shows respect and appreciation. It fosters a sense of teamwork and collaboration. By valuing others, you create an environment where everyone feels included.

Reflecting on how you present yourself can also help. Think about how you come across in different social settings. Are you the center of attention, or do you hang back? Do you speak up or listen more? Self-reflection exercises can be eye-opening. You might discover that you talk a lot or that you rarely share your thoughts. Evaluating your social interactions helps you understand your strengths and areas for improvement. It is like looking in a mirror and seeing the real you. With this insight, you can adjust your approach. You learn to express yourself confidently while leaving space for others. This balance makes social interactions more meaningful and enjoyable.

Embracing Diversity And Cultural Sensitivity In Friendships

Imagine your world like a giant salad bowl. Each ingredient brings something special to the mix. This is what diversity does for friendships. When you have friends from different backgrounds, your life gets richer and more flavorful. These connections help you see the world through different eyes. You learn to appreciate different ways of thinking and living. You become more empathetic, understanding that not everyone sees the world as you do. This empathy helps you grow and become more in tune with others. You see, diversity in friendships is like a bridge. It connects you to experiences and lessons you might never have known.

To really appreciate these differences, you need cultural sensitivity. Think of it as a special lens that helps you see and respect what makes each person unique. It is about acknowledging that everyone has their own story. It means being open to learning about traditions, beliefs, and customs that are different from yours. This sensitivity goes beyond just accepting differences; it is about celebrating them! When you approach friendships with cultural sensitivity, you show that you value what makes others unique. You create a space where everyone feels respected and understood. Ultimately, this respect builds stronger and more meaningful connections.

Building a diverse social circle takes some effort, but it is worth it. Start by seeking out different groups and activities. Join clubs that focus on various interests or attend different cultural events around your community. These places are great for meeting people with different backgrounds. Engage in conversations that explore different cultures. Ask questions and listen to the stories people share. This exposure opens your mind to new ideas and perspectives. It helps you see the world more broadly. It is like traveling to new places without leaving your hometown. Each interaction teaches you something new.

Sometimes, diverse friendships come with challenges. You might face cultural misunderstandings. Maybe a friend says something that feels off, or you misinterpret their actions. When this happens, communication is your best friend. Talk openly and honestly about the misunderstanding. Ask questions to clarify. This approach helps resolve conflicts and strengthens your friendship. Respecting different viewpoints while staying true to your personal values can be a balancing act. It is like walking a tightrope. You want to embrace others' ideas without losing sight of your own beliefs.

Finding this balance helps you grow while still remaining authentic.

Respectful communication is even more necessary across cultures. Avoid past stereotypes and assumptions. They only create barriers and misunderstandings. Instead, approach conversations with pure curiosity. Be willing to learn and explore new concepts. Use inclusive language that respects everyone. When you communicate inclusively, you foster a welcoming environment, and you show that you value everyone's input and experiences. This openness helps build trust and deepens those connections.

Take Carlos and Mei's situation, for example, two teens from different backgrounds who met at a multicultural festival. They bonded over their shared love for music and quickly became friends. As they spent time together, they learned about each other's cultures. Carlos taught Mei about his family's traditions, while Mei introduced Carlos to her favorite foods and holidays. Through these exchanges, they grew closer and gained more understanding of each other's cultural experiences. Their friendship showed them the beauty of diversity and the strength that comes from embracing it.

The Low-Down on Body Language and Social Ques

Imagine you are at a party, music pumping, and people chatting everywhere. You do not hear every word, but you can totally tell who is having fun and who is feeling awkward. That is body language at work. It is the silent conversation happening all around us. Nonverbal cues such as eye contact, posture, and facial expressions can tell us a lot. When someone looks you in the eye, it generally shows they are interested. A slouched posture might mean they are tired or bored. And a smile? Oh, that one can be tricky, but in general, it is the universal nonverbal sign that says, "I am happy!" These signals help us understand how someone feels, even when they do not say a word.

However, context really matters! A wink at a joke might be friendly but come across as strange or unwelcome during a serious meeting. Crossed arms might mean someone is feeling defensive, angry, or maybe just cold. It is like reading a book. The words are the same, but the story changes depending on how you read it. So, pay attention to the situation before jumping to conclusions. Look at the whole picture. Notice how body language fits with what is happening around you. This context helps you interpret signals accurately and avoid misunderstandings. It is like being a detective, piecing together clues to figure out the real story.

Reading social cues is a skill you can improve upon. Start by watching people interact in public places. Notice their movements and expressions. Are they leaning in to listen, or are they looking away? In movies or shows, pay attention to how characters use body language to communicate. These exercises can help sharpen your observation skills. They help you recognize signs of attention, discomfort, and engagement. Understanding these cues can make you more empathetic and aware, and you will start to recognize when someone needs space or when they are open to talking.

Nonverbal communication can support or clash with what we say. Imagine saying, "I am fine," while frowning. The words and expressions do not match. This contradiction can confuse people. On the flip side, mirroring someone's body language can build rapport. If they lean in, you lean in. It shows you are on the same page. However, misreading signals can lead to awkward moments. Maybe you think someone is angry when they're just deep in thought. When in doubt, ask. A simple "Are you okay?" can clarify intentions and prevent misunderstandings.

Improving your own body language starts with self-awareness. Check your posture. Stand tall with shoulders back. It shows confidence. Make eye contact, or close to it, to show that you are genuinely listening. Lean in slightly to show interest. These small changes can make a big difference in how you are perceived. Try self-assessment exercises. Record yourself speaking or ask a friend for feedback. Notice your gestures and expressions. This awareness helps you adjust and improve. You become more conscious of the signals you are sending. It is like tuning an instrument. The more you practice, the more harmonious your interactions become.

Saying No Without The Drama

Imagine you are juggling a mountain of homework, soccer practice, and a family dinner all in one evening. Your friend asks if you can help them with *their* project. You feel the pressure building, but saying "no" seems impossible. Setting boundaries is crucial here. It is like drawing a line in the sand to protect your time and energy. Boundaries keep you from stretching yourself too thin. They help you maintain self-respect and autonomy. When you set boundaries, you let others know what you can and cannot do. It is not about pushing people away. It is about taking care of yourself so you can be your best self for the people you love.

Now, let us talk about saying "no" without causing a scene. It is all about the delivery. Use clear and concise language. Instead of saying, "I do not think I can," try, "I am sorry, I cannot help with that right now." This direct approach leaves no room for misinterpretation. If possible, offer alternative solutions. Say, "I cannot help today, but maybe I can next week," or suggest someone else who might be able to assist. Providing a direct response with other options shows you are still supportive, even if you cannot help directly. It helps soften the blow and keeps the door open for future collaboration.

The fear of disappointing others can make saying "no" feel scary or unfriendly. We worry about letting people down or damaging relationships. But Here is the thing: it is okay to prioritize your needs. Understanding this can help ease the guilt. Remember, you are not being selfish. You are being honest about what you can handle. It is better to say "no" upfront than to say "yes" and struggle to deliver. People will respect you for being genuine. They might even appreciate the clarity you provide. So, give yourself permission to set clear boundaries without all the guilt.

Building your confidence in setting boundaries takes practice. Try role-playing scenarios where saying "no" is necessary. You can do this with a friend or even in front of a mirror.

Practice different ways of declining requests until you find what feels right. You might say, "I appreciate the offer, but I cannot commit right now." The more you practice, the more natural it will become. Soon, saying "no" will feel less like a challenge and more like a normal part of communication. You will find that boundaries actually strengthen your relationships. They create mutual respect and understanding.

Handling Peer Pressure Like A Boss

Peer pressure is like that little voice whispering in your ear, nudging you to do what everyone else is doing. Sometimes, it is loud and direct, like when friends urge you to skip something important for a party. Other times, it is subtle, creeping in through social media. You see posts of friends having fun, and you feel the pull to join in, even when you are not sure you want to. Peer pressure can shape your choices and actions, sometimes without you even noticing. It can make you feel like you need to fit in, even when it goes against what you believe. It is important to know that you are not alone in feeling this way. Many teens and young adults face the same challenges. But Here is the good news: you can resist it.

Standing firm against peer pressure starts with asserting yourself. Being assertive means saying what you think and feel without being aggressive. It is all about finding your voice and using it confidently. Practice saying "no" in a clear and firm way. You do not have to explain yourself or apologize for your answer. A simple "I cannot" or "No, thank you" should be enough. However, developing a personal script for declining unwanted activities can be helpful. Think of it as your go-to response when you are put on the spot. You might say, "I have other plans," or "That is not my thing." Having a ready response can make it easier to stand your ground. It is like having armor to protect your choices.

Surrounding yourself with positive influences can also make a big difference. Choose friends who encourage you to be your best self. Join clubs or groups focused on healthy interests. Whether it is a sports team or a debate club, these environments support positive behavior and help you grow. They provide a safe space where you can be yourself without pressure to conform. When you are with like-minded individuals, you are less likely to feel the need to fit in with negative influences.

Let me share a story about Danny, a teen who loved studying and had big dreams for the future. Danny's friends often pressured him to skip study sessions for parties. It was tempting, but Danny knew what mattered most. He practiced saying "no" and stuck to his plans. He even found friends who shared his academic goals. This support helped him stay focused.

Ultimately, Danny's grades and perseverance helped get him into his dream college. His story shows that sticking to your values pays off. It reminds us that resisting peer pressure is possible, even when it feels hard.

CHAPTER 7: COMMUNICATION > MAKING YOUR VOICE HEARD

"Staying authentic means being true to yourself, no matter the situation."

Imagine you are in a noisy cafeteria where you are trying to share a thought with someone, but it keeps getting drowned out by all the chatter. Finding your voice in these moments can feel like trying to shout over a crowd at a concert. But Here is the secret: your voice matters, and it deserves to be heard. Having a strong personal voice is crucial for expressing who you are and standing up for what you believe in. It is about speaking up when something feels wrong or sharing your ideas without fear. Your voice is your tool for personal empowerment and advocacy.

Speak Up: Finding Your Voice In Conversations

Speaking up in group settings can be nerve-wracking, especially if you are shy or hesitant. But do not worry; there are ways to overcome this. Start by practicing in smaller groups. Gather a few friends and chat about anything— movies, music, or plans for the weekend. This helps build confidence. Use assertive body language, too. Stand tall, make eye contact, and speak clearly. These small changes can make a big difference. They show others that you are confident and ready to contribute.

Over time, these practices will help you feel more comfortable speaking up, even in larger groups.

Crafting clear and concise messages is like organizing your thoughts into a tidy package. It helps you express your ideas without getting lost in the noise. Try mind mapping to organize your thoughts. Write down your main idea in the center and branch out with supporting points.

This visual guide can help you stay on track during conversations. Practicing elevator pitches is another great technique. Imagine you are in an elevator with someone important, and you have only a minute to share your idea. Keep it short, sweet, and to the point. These exercises can help you articulate your thoughts effectively.

Self-reflection is also key to building confidence in speaking. Take a moment to assess your communication skills. What are your strengths?

Maybe you are great at storytelling or asking questions. Identify areas where you can improve. Ask friends for feedback, or try recording yourself speaking. Listen for clarity and tone. This self-assessment helps you understand your unique communication style. It shows you where you shine and where you can grow. Embrace your strengths and work on your weaknesses. Remember, finding your voice is a journey, not a destination. It is about discovering what makes you - you.

Thought Spark: Discover Your Voice

Take a few minutes to reflect on your communication style. Write down three strengths you have when speaking.

Then, jot down one area where you'd like to improve.

Consider asking a friend for feedback on how you speak. What do they notice?

Use this insight to guide your growth as a communicator.

No Cap: Communicating With Honesty And Authenticity

Being honest in communication is an absolute must. It builds trust and makes people believe in *you*. When you speak the truth, others know they can rely on your words. They see you as credible, someone who does not hide behind masks. Imagine having a friend who always tells it like it is. You would trust them, right? That is the power of honesty. It opens doors to deeper connections and makes relationships stronger. People appreciate when you are real with them, even if the truth is not always what they want to hear.

Staying authentic means being true to yourself, no matter the situation. It is about showing the world who you really are, not who you think they want you to be. But how do you do that? Start by being yourself in every situation. If you are silly, be silly. If you are thoughtful, be thoughtful.

Authenticity does not mean you cannot adapt to different situations. You can be genuine while still being flexible. Maybe you tone down the jokes at a formal event yet keep your kind nature. Balance honesty with tact. Share your thoughts, but consider how they might affect others. It is like seasoning food—just the right amount makes it perfect.

Trust me, being authentic is not always easy. Peer pressure and fear of judgment can make you doubt yourself. You might worry about what others think. This fear can be like a heavy door holding you back from being real. It is normal to feel this way, but do not let it control you. Remember, everyone is figuring things out. You are not alone in this. Overcoming fear means facing it head-on, not running away. So, start small. Share a piece of your true self with a trusted friend. Notice how it feels. Each time you do it, you get stronger, and so will the relationship! You learn that being yourself is not only enough but is necessary for your own inner peace.

Authenticity is like glue for relationships. It sticks people together. When you are real, you invite others to be real, too. The act of authenticity creates a bond that goes beyond surface-level interactions. Imagine sharing a genuine laugh or a heartfelt conversation. Those moments build stronger relationships and create memories that last. Authentic interactions are threads, weaving people together and forming connections that can stand the test of time. So, speak truthfully, live authentically, and watch how your relationships bloom!

Leveling Up: Talking To Adults Without Fear

Talking to adults can feel like navigating a maze. You might worry about saying the wrong thing or being misunderstood. It is easy to feel intimidated because adults seem to have all the answers. They sometimes appear strict or serious, which can make opening up tough. But Here is a secret: adults were teens once, too! They have their own fears and doubts in life. Understanding their perspective can help ease your nerves. Adults appreciate honesty and respect. They want to help and guide you. Realizing this can shift how you approach conversations with them. They are not just authority figures; they are also potential mentors and allies.

Starting a conversation with an adult can be less daunting with the right approach. Begin with a simple conversation starter. A question like, "How was your weekend?" or "Did you ever struggle with this subject in school?" can break the ice. These openers show you are interested and respectful.

When the conversation flows, practice active listening. Focus on what they say. Nod or give small verbal cues like "I see" or "That is interesting." These little cues show that you are engaged. Adults notice when you listen, and it builds a bridge of trust. They feel respected and are more likely to listen to you in return.

Building rapport with adults can open doors to valuable advice and needed support. When you communicate openly with parents, teachers, or mentors, you tap into a wealth of experience. They can offer guidance on everything from school projects to personal challenges. Imagine having someone to turn to when you are unsure or need a second opinion. This support system can be a game-changer. It can help you navigate tricky situations with more confidence. Adults appreciate it when you seek their input. It shows maturity and a willingness to learn. More often than not, they will respond with encouragement and insight.

Practicing interactions with adults can help you feel more comfortable. Try role-playing different scenarios. Imagine asking a teacher for help or discussing a problem with a parent. Practice with a friend or in front of a mirror. This exercise lets you explore different ways to express your thoughts. You can experiment with tone, body language, and phrasing. It is like rehearsing for a play. The more you practice, the more natural it feels. You gain confidence, and talking to adults becomes less scary. It becomes an opportunity to connect and learn from those around you.

Comeback Mode: Bounce Back Like A Pro

Imagine you are on a skateboard, cruising right along when suddenly a pebble throws you off balance. You stumble, maybe even fall. But what do you do next? You get back up, dust yourself off, and try again, right?! Well, that is what being emotionally resilient is all about. It is the ability to bounce back from setbacks, to stand up after life knocks you down. For teens, it is ever more crucial. You are navigating school, friendships, and growing up. Resilience helps you keep a positive outlook, even when things get tough. It is like having an emotional trampoline that helps you spring back up after you fall.

Building resilience takes practice, just like learning a new skill. One way to strengthen it is by practicing gratitude. Each day, think about what you are thankful for, no matter how small. It could be a sunny day, good feedback on a report, or a friend who makes you laugh. Gratitude shifts your focus from what is wrong to what is right. It helps you see the silver linings, even in cloudy times. Another technique is setting realistic goals. Break down big tasks into smaller steps. Achieving these gives you a sense of accomplishment. It is like climbing a mountain one step at a time. These small steps build your confidence and resilience over time.

Adopting a growth mindset can also transform how you see challenges. Instead of seeing failures as roadblocks, view them as learning experiences or stepping stones. **Every mistake is a lesson.** It is like a video game - each time you fail a level, you learn something new, preparing you to ace the level on your next try! Embrace these opportunities for growth. Celebrate small victories, too. Maybe you solved a tricky problem or finally stood up for yourself. These wins, no matter how small or big, build your confidence. They remind you of your abilities and encourage you to keep pushing forward.

Consider the story of a teen athlete who faced an injury before a big game. Instead of giving up, they focused on recovery and training. With determination and resilience, they returned stronger, leading their team to victory. History is full of resilient figures, too. Think of those who faced adversity yet persevered. Their stories inspire us to keep going, no matter how tough things get.

Keep It Real: Brain + Feelings

Imagine you are trying to decide whether to join the school soccer team or sign up for the drama club. Both sound fun, but how do you choose? Here is where balancing your brain and your feelings comes in handy. It is all about finding that sweet spot between what your *heart wants* and what your *head knows*. When you balance these two, you make better decisions. Start by weighing the pros and cons. Make a list of what you will gain and what you might miss out on. Consider long-term consequences, too. Will joining the soccer team help you stay fit and make new friends? Or will the drama club boost your confidence and creativity? Thinking ahead helps you see the bigger picture.

Evaluating decisions can feel overwhelming, but it does not have to be. Break it down step by step. Try creating a decision matrix. Draw a grid with your options on one side and factors like time, cost, and fun on the other.

Score each factor and see which option scores higher. This visual approach makes it clear which choice fits best. Do not forget to seek advice from trusted mentors or peers. They might offer insights you had not considered. Sometimes, a fresh perspective can make all the difference. It is like getting a second opinion before deciding what movie to watch.

Emotions play a big role in decision-making, too. They are not just there to confuse you. When managed wisely, they can guide you. Intuition, or that gut feeling, is your brain's way of using past experiences to make a choice. Trust it, but do not let it take over completely. Use it along with logic.

Imagine you are deciding between two friends to invite to a concert. Your gut tells you one might enjoy it more, but your brain reminds you the other could use a fun night out. Balancing these inputs helps you make a choice that feels right.

Think about Jake, a student deciding between extracurricular activities. He loved both basketball and art club. He thought about his goals and realized that the art club would help his future career path. But he did not ignore his love for sports. He found a way to balance both, playing basketball on weekends. By considering both his emotions and logic, he found a solution that worked.

Staying Solid In Group Situations

Have you ever been in a group project meeting, and things got super intense? When everyone is talking at once, it is easy to feel lost in the chaos. This is where self-regulation comes in. It is all about keeping your cool and not letting emotions take over. In a group setting, self-control is key. It helps you maintain composure when disagreements pop up. Maybe someone disagrees with your idea, and you feel your face heat up. Instead of snapping back, take a deep breath. Self-regulation means listening to all voices, even when you do not agree. It is about giving everyone a fair chance to speak. Doing this keeps the environment respectful and productive.

To create a positive team dynamic, start by setting group norms. These are the rules everyone agrees to follow. That might include things like taking turns speaking, staying on topic, or respecting each other's opinions. When everyone knows the rules, it is easier to stay on track. Rotating leadership roles is another great strategy. It builds responsibility and lets everyone experience leading and following. Perhaps this week, you lead the discussion, and next week, someone else does. This shared responsibility helps everyone feel valued and heard. It also teaches you to see things from different perspectives, which is a valuable skill in any group setting.

Managing stress in a team can be tricky, especially when deadlines are looming. Group mindfulness exercises can help. Before starting a meeting, take a few minutes to practice deep breathing together. It sets a calm tone and helps everyone focus. Establish clear goals and responsibilities so everyone knows what they are working toward, reducing confusion and stress. When everyone understands their role, the team functions more smoothly. It is like being in a band where everyone knows their part.

Together, you create harmony.

Squash The Beef: Turning Drama Into Growth

Conflict resolution is a powerful tool for any relationship. It is what turns drama into something positive. When you resolve a conflict, you do not just stop the arguing; you also learn to understand each other better. It is about finding peace and building stronger connections. Conflicts can pop up anywhere—at school, at work, at home, or with friends. But knowing how to handle them constructively can make all the difference. It is like having a tool that transforms shouting matches into meaningful conversations. When you resolve things well, everyone wins. You feel heard, and so does the other person. It is a win-win situation that leaves everyone feeling better.

So, how do you actually resolve a conflict? First, you need to find out what is really causing the problem. Sometimes, the real issue is hiding beneath the surface. Maybe it is not about the last slice of pizza but about feeling left out. Once you understand the root cause, you can address it head-on. Next, communicate your feelings calmly and assertively. Use "I" statements to express how you feel *without* blaming the other person. Doing so keeps

the conversation open and respectful. It is not about attacking; it is about sharing and understanding. You will be surprised at how smoothly things go when you talk with honesty and kindness.

Compromise plays a big role in resolving conflicts. It is like meeting each other halfway. You both give a little to reach a solution that works for everyone. Brainstorm together to find solutions that satisfy both sides. You may agree to alternate who picks the movie or split chores in a way that feels fair. Compromise does not mean losing. It means finding common ground. It shows that you value the relationship more than the argument.

When you work together to solve a problem, you strengthen your bond. You learn to respect and appreciate each other's perspectives. It is like growing stronger together; one resolved conflict at a time.

Take the story of a group project dispute. It started with disagreements over who did what. Tensions ran high, but they decided to sit down and talk.

They identified the real issue: a lack of communication. By sharing their feelings using 'I' statements and brainstorming together, they found a way forward. They divided tasks more clearly and supported each other. In the end, not only did they finish the project successfully, but they also became closer as friends. This shows that with the right approach, conflicts can lead to growth and connection.

CHAPTER 8: MOTIVATION > FUELING YOUR INNER DRIVE

"It is not just about what you do. It is about WHY you do it!"

Have you ever tried pushing a door that clearly says "pull"? That is what life feels like sometimes. We push and push, yet somehow, nothing seems to budge. Motivation is a key that unlocks that door and makes everything feel just a bit easier. So, how do you find that key - how do you go about discovering what truly drives you? Think back to a time when you felt on top of the world ... maybe you aced a project or nailed a dance routine. What inside of you fueled that fire? Reflect on those successes. Was it the thrill of competition or the joy of learning something new? These moments are breadcrumbs leading to your motivators, your fuel to succeed.

Next, consider activities that bring you joy and fulfillment. Is it painting, playing guitar, or coding? Whatever it is, that joy is a clue. When you love what you do, motivation follows naturally. It is like fuel that never runs out. Your emotions can be powerful motivators, too. Passion ignites a spark.

When you are passionate about an activity, you put your heart into it. It is not just about the end goal. It is about enjoying the ride. It is the feeling you get when you are so into something that hours just fly by without you noticing. That is passion-driven motivation, and it is golden!

Finding Your Why: What Drives You?

Let us dive deeper. Aligning motivation with your values can give you a sustained drive. Values are like your personal compass. They guide your choices and actions. Take some time for introspection. What matters most to you? Is it kindness, creativity, or helping others? Identifying these values helps you focus on what truly matters. When your actions align with your values, you feel more fulfilled. It is like finding the perfect playlist for your mood. Everything just clicks. This alignment keeps you motivated, even on tough days. You know you are moving in the right direction.

Consider Bonnie, a teen with a heart for animals. She loved spending time with them and wanted to make a difference. So, she started volunteering at an animal shelter. Her love for animals became her "why." It fueled her efforts, making even the hard tasks feel worthwhile. Her story shows that finding your "why" can propel you forward. It gives you purpose and direction. It is not just about what you do. It is about why you do it. When you find that reason, motivation becomes a friend, not a struggle.

Thought Spark: Discover Your "Why"

Grab a notebook, or use the space below and jot down three activities that make you happy.

Next, write down why they matter to you.

Look for patterns.

What do these activities have in common?

Use this reflection to uncover your motivators.

Goals On Fleek: Setting And Achieving Milestones

Setting goals is like plotting a course for a road trip. You need a clear destination and the steps to get there. That is where SMART goals come in. They help you create a roadmap that makes sense. SMART stands for Specific, Measurable, Achievable, Relevant, and Time-bound. Think of it like this: if you want to improve your math grades, be specific. Aim to increase your average from a B to an A. Make it measurable by setting a target score for each test. Ensure it is achievable by considering your current skills. Keep it relevant, focusing on subjects that impact your overall performance. Lastly, set a time frame, like by the end of the semester. This structure keeps your goals clear and within reach. Be sure to write it down and check in on your progress regularly!

Now, let us break it down further. Imagine your goal is to run a mile in under ten minutes. That sounds big, right? But by breaking it into smaller pieces, it becomes more manageable. Start with a step-by-step plan. Begin by jogging for shorter distances and gradually increase your speed and distance. Each week, aim to shave a few seconds off your time. Celebrate small victories along the way. This approach turns a daunting task into a series of achievable steps, making progress feel natural and less overwhelming. It is like building a Lego castle one brick at a time. Each piece matters, and together, they create something amazing.

Flexibility is key in this process. Life loves to throw curveballs, and your plans might need tweaking. You might get injured or find it hard to keep up with a new routine. That is okay. Being adaptable means recognizing when a goal needs adjusting; maybe you can adjust the timeline for success or modify the smaller steps therein. Staying flexible helps keep you on track even when things do not go as planned. It is about rolling with the punches and finding new ways forward. Think of it as adjusting your sails when the wind changes direction. You still reach your destination, just by a slightly different route, and that is perfectly OK!

Take Grace, a student with dreams of earning a scholarship for college. She set specific goals for maintaining a certain GPA and participating in extracurricular activities. She tackled each requirement with determination, breaking them into smaller tasks. When unexpected challenges cropped up, like a tough class or a new club responsibility, she adjusted her schedule.

Her consistent effort paid off, and she reached her scholarship milestone. Grace's story shows that with clear goals, a flexible mindset, and persistent effort, you can achieve what you set out to do. Her journey is proof that any milestone is possible with the right approach.

Get Stuff Done: Overcoming Task Paralysis

Ever find yourself staring at a mountain of work, not even knowing where to start? It is like standing at the edge of a diving board, frozen in place. You are not alone. Procrastination is the sneaky culprit. It loves to whisper, "Why do today what you can put off until tomorrow?" But face it: diving headfirst into procrastination gets you absolutely nowhere.

Sometimes, fear of failure or the pressure to be perfect makes you hesitate. What if you do not get it right? Or the task may feel so big that you do not know where to begin. It is like trying to eat an entire pizza in one bite—not a good idea!

It is time to change the game plan. Enter time-management techniques. The Pomodoro Technique can be your new best friend. It is about setting a timer for a short, focused work session, like 25 minutes, followed by a break.

During those minutes, you work on one task; no distractions are allowed. When the timer rings, take a short break. Repeat this cycle, and soon, you will find that tasks do not seem as daunting. Scheduling regular breaks keeps your brain fresh and prevents burnout. It is like hitting refresh on your mental browser. Suddenly, that mountain of work seems more like a series of small hills.

Accountability can be a powerful motivator. Find a study buddy or accountability partner. Share your goals and check in with each other. It is like having a gym buddy but for your brain. You motivate each other and celebrate victories, no matter how small. Knowing someone else is counting on you can keep you on track and make the process more fun. Plus, working with someone else can bring in fresh ideas and perspectives. They might spot something you missed or suggest a quicker way to tackle a problem.

Celebrating Wins: Big And Small

Imagine finally finishing that huge puzzle you have been working on. The moment you place the last piece; you feel a rush of pride. Celebrating wins, both big and small, is like that. It boosts your self-esteem and keeps you going. It does not matter if it is a major event or just getting out of bed on a tough day. Every achievement deserves a moment of recognition.

Celebrating reinforces positive behavior, making you want to keep reaching for more. It is like giving yourself a high-five for a job well done. This celebration is not just fun; it is key to staying motivated.

So, how do you celebrate? Get creative! Host a small get-together with friends to mark a milestone. It does not have to be fancy—a simple movie night or picnic works wonders. Or treat yourself to something special. Maybe it is a favorite snack or some time playing your go-to video game.

Even a short walk in the park can feel refreshing. Celebrations do not have to be grand. They just need to remind you that you have accomplished something. It is these little rewards that keep you motivated and excited for what comes next.

Reflecting on your achievements can be just as powerful. Take some time to journal about what you accomplished. Write down the steps you took and what worked well. This reflection helps you understand the journey and prepares you for future goals. It shows you what strategies helped you succeed and what you might change next time. You might discover a pattern or find new strengths you did not realize you had. Journaling is like a conversation with yourself. It is a way to celebrate not just the achievement but the growth that came with it.

Let us talk about Zach, a teen who celebrates academic milestones with family traditions. Each time Zach aces a test or finishes a project, the family gathers for a homemade pizza night.

They share stories and laughter, making Zach feel valued and supported. This tradition not only marks Zach's achievements but also strengthens family bonds. It is a reminder that accomplishments are worth celebrating, no matter how small they might seem. Zach's story shows how turning achievements into traditions can create lasting memories and motivation.

Staying Inspired: Keep The Motivation Alive

Picture this: you are on a hike when you suddenly reach a breathtaking view. That rush of awe and energy is inspiration at work. Inspiration breathes life into motivation, making the impossible seem possible. So, how do you find it? Start by seeking role models or mentors who light that spark. Maybe a teacher or supervisor who believes in you or a family member whose story has moved you. Their journey can guide you, offering new perspectives and encouragement. They can show you what really is possible, even when it feels tough or impossible.

Finding new hobbies or interests can reignite passion and excitement. Have you ever tried something new and felt that thrill of excitement? New experiences can open doors to creativity and inspiration. Explore different activities that catch your attention. You never know what might become your next big passion. Reading biographies of inspiring figures can also revitalize motivation. Discover the stories of people who overcame challenges and achieved greatness. Their victories and struggles can remind you that everyone starts somewhere. You will learn that setbacks are a part of the process, not the end of it.

Continuous learning and growth also fuel motivation. Think of it as watering a plant—constant care keeps it thriving. Enroll in workshops or classes to gain new skills. Whether it is a coding workshop or a photography class, learning something new keeps you engaged. It pushes you to grow and adapt, broadening your horizons. Each new skill or piece of knowledge adds to your toolkit, preparing you for whatever comes next. The excitement of learning something fresh can keep your motivation alive and kicking. It shows you that there is always more to discover and achieve.

Stress SOS: Quick Fixes For Overwhelming Moments

Life can feel like a juggling act. You have got school, work, social life, and family all throwing balls in your direction. Sometimes, it feels like you are going to drop them all. Stress kicks in, and suddenly, everything seems too much. Academic pressure is a big one. With tests, projects, and homework piling up, it is like a never-ending mountain to climb. Then, there is the social side. Friends, parties, and the latest drama can add to the stress. Do not forget family expectations. They want the best for you, but sometimes, it feels like the weight of the world rests on your shoulders.

When stress hits, quick relief can be a lifesaver. These simple acts pull you away from stress and help you find calm:

> Start with deep breathing. Take a slow breath in, hold it, and then let it out. Do it a few times. It slows your heart rate and calms your mind.

> Progressive muscle relaxation is another trick. Tense each muscle group one at a time, then relax. Start with your toes and work up. It is like hitting reset on your body.

> Focus on the present moment. Take stock of each of your senses: take note of what you hear around you, feel how your clothes touch your skin, breathe in the scents that are nearby, look out a window or at a picture of nature, and take a drink or bite of food to savor and enjoy the flavors as they move through your mouth.

Changing how you talk to yourself can also ease stress. Positive self-talk is your friend. Instead of thinking, "I cannot do this," try, "I have got this." It is a tiny shift, but it makes a big difference. Use affirmations like, "I am capable" or "I can handle what comes my way." Reframe negative thoughts. If you think, "I am going to fail," change it to, "I'll do my best, and that is enough." These tweaks in your inner dialogue can make stress feel less heavy.

Creating a personal SOS plan helps manage stress when it shows up. Start by spotting your stress signals. Maybe your heart races or your jaw tightens. Write these down. Then, craft a step-by-step response plan. Include things like deep breathing, taking a walk, or talking to someone you trust. Having this plan ready means you can act fast when stress begins to bubble up. It is like having a first-aid kit for your mind.

By recognizing stress, using quick relief techniques, and building a personal plan, you can handle the chaos. Remember, stress doesn't have to control you. With the right tools, you can keep it in check and stay grounded.

Moving forward, we will explore ways to build resilience and turn challenges into opportunities for growth.

CHAPTER 9: NAVIGATING CHANGE > THRIVING IN TRANSITIONS

"You don't need to change to be liked. Embrace your uniqueness!"

Have you ever tried surfing? At first, you wobble on the board, trying not to crash into the waves. But with practice, you start to balance, even riding the waves with a grin. That is a lot like dealing with change. It can feel wobbly and uncertain, but it leads to growth. Change is natural. It is as constant as the sunrise. Whether you are moving to a new city or starting at a new school, change brings new experiences. These transitions can feel daunting at first, but they can also open doors to exciting opportunities.

When you move to a new place, everything feels unfamiliar. You are unsure where things are or how to fit in. But this is an opportunity to explore new possibilities. You might discover a new hobby or meet friends who share your interests. Embracing change with an open mind allows you to learn and grow. Practicing flexibility is key. Instead of resisting change, welcome it. Focus on the positives. Think of the fresh start and the adventures that come with it.

Change often brings mixed emotions. You might feel anxious about leaving behind what is familiar. It is okay to feel unsure about the future. These feelings are totally normal. It is managing them that is important. Try focusing on what excites you about the change. It could be the chance to reinvent yourself or explore new places. This anticipation can help balance the uncertainty. It is like being on a carnival ride. The ride can be scary, but the thrill is usually worth it.

Thought Spark: Riding The Waves Of Change

Take a moment to reflect on a recent change in your life.

What were your initial feelings?

What opportunities did it bring?

Write down how you adapted and what you learned from the experience.

This reflection helps you see change as a chance to grow and thrive.

The Rollercoaster Ride Of Puberty

Puberty is a time when your body and mind feel like they are on a wild rollercoaster ride. One minute, you are laughing with friends, and the next, you are feeling upset or angry for no reason. These situations happen because hormones are flooding your body. They affect your emotions and can cause mood swings. It is like your brain is rewiring itself, trying to figure things out. This emotional volatility is normal. You might feel like you are on a mood rollercoaster, but knowing that it is part of growing up can help. Remember, you are not alone in feeling this way. Many teens experience the same rollercoaster of emotional changes.

Managing these intense emotions can be tricky, but there are ways to help. Breathing exercises are a great start. When you feel overwhelmed, take a deep breath in, hold it for a moment, and then slowly exhale. Repeat this a few times. It helps calm your racing heart and clears your mind. Journaling is another useful tool. Write down your thoughts and feelings. It is like talking to a friend who really gets you. Putting your emotions on paper can help you see them more clearly. It is a way to release stress without keeping it bottled up inside.

During puberty, it is crucial to practice self-compassion. Be kind to yourself. When you make a mistake, remember that it is a part of the learning process. Instead of beating yourself up, try saying, "It is okay; I am doing my best." This simple shift in mindset can make a big difference.

Talking about these changes can also help. Find someone you trust, like a parent, teacher, or friend. Start a conversation with something like, "I have been feeling different lately. Can we talk?" Being open about your feelings makes it easier to handle them. It also lets others know how to support you. Identifying supportive individuals in your life can make this ride less bumpy.

New School, New Friends: Making Connections

Starting at a new school can feel like stepping into a different world. Everything seems unfamiliar, from the bustling hallways to the way classes are organized. It can be overwhelming but do not worry. There are ways to find your footing. Start by getting to know the layout. Find out where your classes are, the cafeteria, and the gym. Knowing where things are can make the school feel more like home. Also, take time to understand the school rules and norms. These are the unwritten codes that guide how things work. They help you blend in and feel more at ease.

Now, let us talk about making friends. It might feel scary at first, but joining clubs or sports teams can help. These are great places to meet people who share your interests. Whether it is the art club, soccer team, or debate group, you will find others who get you. Be proactive in starting conversations. A simple "Hi, I am new here. What is your name?" can go a long way. People are often more welcoming than you expect. They might be curious about you, too. Building a social network takes time, but each small step brings you closer to finding your tribe.

Starting over can come with challenges. Feeling lonely or out of place is perfectly normal. It is okay to miss your old friends and familiar routines. But remember, you are not alone. Many teens feel this way when they start fresh. Try to focus on the opportunities ahead. Handle the pressure to fit in by staying true to yourself. You do not need to change to be liked. Embrace your uniqueness. It sets you apart and helps you find friends who appreciate you for who you are.

Navigating New Environments: From School To College

Stepping into college for the first time is like entering a whole new world. It is exciting and a bit daunting. Gone are the familiar faces and routines of high school. Instead, you are in a place where the possibilities and people are endless. College dynamics are different. Classes may be larger, and professors expect you to be more independent. There is more freedom, but with that comes the need to manage your time and responsibilities. For many, it is the first taste of living away from home. This new independence can feel thrilling and overwhelming at the same time. Suddenly, *you* are in charge of everything from laundry to meals. It is a lot to handle, but it is also a chance to grow and learn to stand on your own.

To adapt to this new environment, start by taking advantage of orientation sessions and campus tours. These are designed to help you get familiar with the campus layout and resources. Knowing where the library, gym, and dining hall are can make you feel more at home. Joining clubs or student groups is another great way to settle in. Whether it is a sport, hobby, or academic interest, these groups help you meet people with similar passions. Plus, they provide a sense of community and belonging in a vast sea of students. Getting involved early can make the transition smoother and more enjoyable.

Building a support network is crucial in college. You will need people to lean on, whether it is for study help or just to hang out. Find a mentor, maybe a professor or an upper-level student, who can guide you through the maze of college. Their advice and experience can be invaluable. Creating study groups with classmates can also be helpful. It gives you a chance to share ideas and tackle tough subjects together. Having a group of friends who understand what you are going through makes college life way more manageable and fun.

College is a melting pot of cultures and ideas. Embrace the diversity around you. Attend cultural events and participate in exchange programs. These experiences broaden your horizons and help you appreciate different perspectives. They are opportunities to learn more about the world and yourself. Being open to new experiences can transform your college years into a time of true discovery and personal growth.

The Transition Tango: Moving From School To The Real World

Stepping out of school feels like standing at the edge of a diving board. You are excited about the plunge but nervous about what may be below. Moving from school to work or further studies can bring a rush of emotions. There is the thrill of new beginnings, the chance to explore, and the fear of the unknown. You might wonder if you will succeed or if you are ready for the challenges ahead. It is normal to feel a mix of eagerness and anxiety.

Familiar routines fade, replaced by new expectations. This emotional rollercoaster is a part of growing up. It is about leaving one world behind and entering another world that is full of opportunities and uncertainties.

To handle this wave of change, you will need some strategies. Visualization can help. Picture yourself succeeding in your new role. Imagine the steps you will take. This positive outlook can boost your confidence. Creating a transition plan can also ease your mind. Break down your goals into small, actionable steps. If you are starting a job, the first step might be learning the commute or mastering a new skill. Having a plan gives you direction and makes the unknown feel less daunting. It is like having a map when you are in a new city. You know where you are headed, even if the path seems long.

Adaptability is key. Life does not always go as planned, and that is okay. Being open to change helps you thrive in new settings. Consider Laney, who moved from a small town to a bustling city for a job. She embraced the chaos, learned something new each day, and found her rhythm. Exercises

like trying new activities or meeting new people can build adaptability. They teach you to handle surprises with ease. By staying flexible, you are ready for whatever comes your way.

Setting realistic expectations helps ground you. The real world is not always like the movies. It is full of ups and downs. Reflect on your goals and what you want to achieve. Talk to someone who has been there, like a professional or mentor. Their insights can give you a clearer picture of what to expect. These conversations can help balance your dreams with reality, guiding you toward what is possible.

Coping With Loss And Disappointment

Loss can feel like a heavy backpack you carry around. Maybe it is the end of a friendship that once felt unbreakable, a relationship that fizzled out when you least expected it, or even the passing of someone close. These moments can hit hard, leaving you with a mix of emotions like sadness, anger, and confusion. It is normal to feel these things. Disappointment, too, can sting, especially when expectations are not met. You might have worked hard for something, only to watch it slip away. These feelings can seem overwhelming, like a storm you cannot escape. But understanding them is the first step in lightening that load.

Journaling can be a powerful way to deal with these emotions. Writing down how you feel allows you to process those feelings in your own time. It is like having a conversation with yourself, where no one interrupts. You can pour out your heart on the page, and it does not judge - nor should you, as this can actually bring clarity and relief if you allow yourself to let it go after writing it down. Reaching out to friends or family is also helpful.

Talking to someone you trust can give you a fresh perspective. They may offer you comfort, advice, or simply a listening ear. Knowing you are not alone can make a world of difference.

Resilience is about bouncing back when life knocks you down. It is not about pretending everything is fine. Instead, it is about finding strength in tough times. Every loss or disappointment carries a lesson. You could learn more about what you truly value or discover a totally new path that you had not considered. These experiences can be stepping stones to something greater within.

Adulting 101: Confidence In Handling New Responsibilities

"Adulting" is a buzzword you hear a lot, but what does it really mean? It is about stepping up and taking on new responsibilities as you grow. You might feel a mix of excitement and dread. Suddenly, you have to manage things like finances, make big decisions, and maybe even cook your meals. These tasks can feel overwhelming at first, but they are key to building confidence. Successfully handling responsibilities boosts your self-esteem. You start to realize, "Hey, I can do this!" Everyday responsibilities like budgeting or deciding your future path are part of the adulting package.

Mastering responsibilities is like adding badges to your sash of life. Each task you tackle makes you more independent and self-reliant. To handle tasks confidently, break them into smaller steps. Prioritize which tasks need attention first. This approach makes even the biggest challenges feel manageable. Proactive planning is your secret weapon. Set clear goals and create an action plan. For example, if you want to save money, set a monthly savings target. These exercises help you stay on track and build confidence with each achievement.

Staying organized is crucial. Use time management tools like planners or apps to keep track of tasks. Personal systems, like a to-do list, can help you manage responsibilities efficiently. Setting both short and long-term goals keeps you focused. Reflective learning is also vital. Instead of seeing mistakes as failures, view them as opportunities to learn and improve. This growth mindset turns setbacks into stepping stones toward your own success.

Independence is a double-edged sword. It offers freedom but also brings emotional challenges. You might feel excited about making your own choices but also anxious about the unknown. Finding a balance is key. Seek guidance when needed. Join clubs or find a role model who inspires you.

Mentorship and peer support can provide valuable advice and make adulting less daunting. They remind you that while independence is important, you do not have to navigate it all alone.

Planning For The Future: Setting Long-Term Goals

Think of your life as a blank canvas, waiting for your brushstrokes to create a masterpiece. Setting long-term goals is like sketching the outline of that painting. It gives you direction, helping you see where you want to go in life. Whether it is aiming for a dream career or planning your next big adventure, having a vision is key. It helps you understand what steps you need to take to reach those aspirations. Think of it as a roadmap, guiding you through the twists and turns of life. With a clear vision, you are more likely to stay focused and motivated.

To make those big dreams a reality, break them down into smaller, actionable steps. Imagine you are building a sandcastle. Instead of trying to create it all at once, you start with one bucket of sand at a time. Each step brings you closer to your goal. Setting timelines is also crucial. It helps track your progress and keeps you accountable. When you see milestones approaching, you will feel a sense of achievement. And when things do not go as planned, do not stress - stay flexible. Sometimes, goals need tweaking. Be open to adjusting them as your circumstances change. New opportunities might pop up, leading you down exciting paths you had not considered before.

Let us talk about Jason. He dreamed of becoming a marine biologist. He set his long-term goal and mapped out the steps:

1. Ace science classes,
2. Join the biology club,
3. And volunteer at the local aquarium.

Along the way, he discovered a passion for environmental conservation. Jason adjusted his goals to include this new interest. His journey shows that staying flexible and open can lead to unexpected and rewarding outcomes.

Planning for the future is about setting a course but also being ready to explore new horizons along the way.

△△△

CHAPTER 10: BUILDING STRONG RELATIONSHIPS

Picture this: you are at a school dance, and you have finally gathered the courage to ask your crush to dance. Your heart's racing faster than a YouTube video on double speed. Romantic relationships can feel exciting, but they can also be a bit scary if you do not know how to handle them. That is where emotional intelligence steps in. It is like having a cheat sheet for relationships, helping you understand your own feelings and those of your partner. Imagine knowing exactly what to say when your partner is upset or how to express your feelings without starting World War III.

Bae Basics: Emotional Intelligence In Romantic Relationships

In any relationship, being aware of your own emotions is crucial. It helps you stay calm and think before you act. When you know how you feel, you can communicate better. Think about it like this: if you are frustrated, you can say, "I am feeling overwhelmed right now," instead of lashing out. This type of wording helps your partner understand and support you. Empathy is another biggie. It is about putting yourself in your partner's shoes. When they are upset, try to feel what they feel. It can be as simple as listening without jumping in with advice. Sometimes, just saying, "I get it, that sounds tough," can make a huge difference. And when you do disagree, remember to practice empathy. It is easy to get defensive, but try seeing things from your partner's side. This opens the door to understanding and compromise.

Communication is the glue that holds relationships together. Without it, things fall apart. One way to improve communication is through active listening exercises. Sit down with your partner and take turns sharing your thoughts. While one talks, the other listens without interrupting. Then, repeat back what you heard to make sure you understood. This exercise helps deepen your understanding of each other. Also, be clear about your needs and boundaries. If you need some alone time, say it. If something bothers you, speak up. Clear communication prevents misunderstandings and helps keep things smooth.

While sharing your life with someone special is amazing, it is important to keep your individuality intact. Balance your relationship with personal growth. Pursue hobbies that light you up, whether it is painting, playing guitar, or hiking. This keeps you energized and happy. Encourage your partner to do the same. Independent friendships are important, too. They give you space to be yourself and bring fresh energy into the relationship.

Remember, it is okay to hang out with friends without your partner. It strengthens your bond and keeps things fresh. Conflict is natural in any relationship. It is how you handle it that matters. When a disagreement pops up, focus on resolving it constructively.

Compromise is key. Think of it like sharing a pizza. Maybe one of you loves pepperoni, and the other is all about veggies. Find a way to split the toppings. Negotiation is not about winning; it is about finding a solution that works for both. Be sure to use "I" statements during discussions.

Instead of blaming, say, "I feel hurt when..." This shifts the focus to your feelings and encourages understanding rather than defensiveness.

Family Ties: Navigating Family Dynamics

Imagine you are sitting at the dinner table, and suddenly, a debate about who forgot to take out the trash turns into an epic family saga. Families are like that—a mix of love, chaos, and shared history. Understanding family roles and dynamics can make a big difference. Every family has its patterns, like who is the peacemaker, the jokester, or the one always running late.

Recognizing these roles helps you see why people act the way they do. It is like solving a puzzle. Each piece represents a family member's style, and together, they show how the family communicates. Generational differences play a part, too. Your parents grew up in a different world, with different tech and trends, which can cause misunderstandings. Knowing this can help you bridge those gaps.

Communication is key to keeping family ties strong, and having family meetings can be super helpful. Try to set a time when everyone is relaxed, maybe after dinner or during a weekend breakfast. Make it a safe space where everyone gets to speak without being interrupted. Active listening is important here. When someone talks, give them your full attention. Nod, smile, or even paraphrase what they said to show you are listening. It is like saying, "I hear you, and I care." These meetings can help clear the air and bring everyone closer.

Conflicts happen in every family. The trick is handling them without drama. Mediation is one way to do this. If two family members are at odds, act as a neutral party to help them see each other's perspectives. Encourage them to talk about their feelings without pointing fingers. Setting boundaries is also crucial. Maybe you need a quiet hour after school or a heads-up before guests come over. Communicate these needs clearly. Boundaries help everyone understand and respect each other's space and feelings.

Gratitude can hold families together. It is easy to take your family for granted, but a little appreciation goes a long way. Try writing gratitude letters. It could be a simple note to your mom for her awesome cooking or to your sibling for lending you their favorite game. These letters show love and gratitude. Family appreciation rituals can be fun, too. Perhaps every Friday night, you all share one thing you are thankful for. This ritual strengthens bonds and reminds every one of the good stuff, even during tough times.

Teacher Talk: Building Respectful Relationships With Educators

Respectful communication with teachers can open doors to a better learning experience. When you approach teachers for help, it shows you care about your education. Whether it is asking about a tricky math problem or seeking advice on a project, being proactive helps build rapport. Participating actively in class also makes a big impact. Sharing ideas, raising your hand, or even just nodding along can show teachers that you are engaged. It is like giving them a thumbs-up that says, "I am here, and I am ready to learn."

Improving communication with teachers starts with preparation. Before class, jot down questions you might have. It shows that you are thinking ahead and ready to dive into the lesson. When you need to reach out, consider sending a professional email. Keep it clear and concise, like, "Hi, Mr. Smith, I need help with the homework. Can we chat after class?" It saves time and shows respect. This kind of communication helps you stand out as a student who takes their work seriously. Teachers appreciate that, and it is a good way to build a positive relationship.

These strong relationships with educators can be game-changers. Teachers are more than just authority figures; they are mentors who can guide you. They can offer valuable career advice and help you see potential paths for your future. By building a positive connection, you open up opportunities for mentorship, which means having someone who cheers you on and helps you grow. They might even write you a killer recommendation letter someday. This support can boost both your academic success and personal development.

Sometimes, misunderstandings happen. Maybe you did not agree with a grade, or you felt misheard. It is important to handle these situations respectfully. Request a private meeting with your teacher. It shows maturity and willingness to resolve issues. During the meeting, stay calm and express your feelings clearly.

Remember to use "I" statements, like "I felt confused about the feedback on my essay." This approach helps clarify things without pointing fingers or escalating the situation. Teachers appreciate kindness and honesty and are often willing to help work things out.

Squad Dynamics: Managing Group Conflicts

Imagine you are doing a group project, and everyone has their own idea of how to get things done. Some want to dive right in, while others prefer a more laid-back approach. It is like trying to mix oil and water. Here is where understanding group dynamics can help. Emotional Intelligence plays a big role in making group work smoother. First, recognize the roles people naturally take on. Maybe one friend is the planner who keeps everyone on track, while another is the creative thinker. Be appreciative of these roles and contributions and encourage everyone to join in. Make sure each voice is heard, even the quietest one. This inclusivity can turn a chaotic mess into a well-oiled machine.

Conflicts are bound to pop up. Maybe someone feels left out, or two people clash over differing ideas. Address these issues head-on to keep the peace. Facilitate group discussions where everyone gets a chance to speak, set ground rules like no interrupting, and listen with respect. If things get heated, mediation can help. Act as a neutral party to guide the conversation. Encourage everyone to share their feelings without blaming others. This approach can turn disagreements into productive discussions. It is like turning down the volume and tuning into understanding.

Setting clear group norms and expectations can prevent misunderstandings. Work together to define shared values and rules. Establish group goals collaboratively. Whether it is finishing a project or winning a game, having a shared vision keeps everyone focused. These guidelines act as a roadmap, showing the way forward and reducing bumps along the way. They help everyone stay on the same page and work towards a common goal.

Reflect on group experiences to learn and improve. After a project, take time to discuss what went well and what could be better. Group reflection exercises help identify strengths and areas for improvement.

Analyze examples of successful teamwork. Maybe a past project went smoothly because everyone communicated openly. Use these insights to guide future group work. Look at what worked and what did not. This reflection helps you grow as a team member and improves future interactions. It is like looking in a mirror to see where you can shine brighter next time.

Peer Pressure Navigation: Staying True In Tough Situations

Imagine you are at a party, and everyone is daring you to try something you are not comfortable with. Peer pressure is a master at sneaking in, not just in high school but well into adulthood. In college, friends might push you to skip studying for a night out. At work, colleagues could pressure you into cutting corners on tasks. It can feel like trying to swim against the tide. The urge to fit in and say "yes" to everything can be overwhelming. But staying true to your values is important, like having a solid compass in a storm, guiding you to make choices that feel right for you.

How do you stand firm when the pressure is on? Start with some role-playing exercises. They might feel silly, but practicing assertiveness helps. Picture a friend playing the role of someone pressuring you. Respond with confidence, saying, "No, thanks, I am good." Developing a personal code of ethics can be your shield. Write down what you believe in and what lines you will not cross. Keep it somewhere you can see it, serving as a reminder of who you are and what you stand for. It is your personal set of rules designed to help you stay grounded when others try to sway you.

Self-awareness is your secret weapon in resisting peer pressure. Knowing yourself means understanding *your* core beliefs and values.

Self-assessment quizzes can also guide you. They help you identify your strengths and areas for growth. With this self-awareness, you are better equipped to stand firm in your decisions. It is like having a mirror that reflects your true self, making it harder for others to pull you away from it.

Building a supportive network is key. Surround yourself with people who respect and support your individuality. These are your allies. They will not pressure you to change but will encourage you to be yourself and to grow. Look for these allies in both social and professional circles.

Relationships built on mutual respect and shared values are priceless. These connections offer a safe space where you can be true to yourself without fear of judgment, much like having a safety net catching you when you feel tempted to stray from your path.

Thought Spark: Understanding Your Core Beliefs And Values

Spend some time writing about what truly matters to you.

What are your non-negotiables?

Who do you want to be?

Empathy And Respect: The Cornerstones Of Lasting Relationships

Imagine trying to have a conversation where you are speaking different languages. That is what it is like without empathy in relationships. Empathy is all about understanding and really feeling what someone else is going through. It is about seeing the world through their eyes. Why is this important? Because when you understand someone's feelings, it makes your connection stronger. You start to get why they do what they do, and it helps you respond in a way that shows you care. Think about your best friend being upset. Instead of saying, "Get over it," you might say, "I am here for you." That simple shift can make a world of difference.

Respect is the flip side of empathy. It is about valuing what others think and feel. When you respect someone, you build trust. Trust is another glue that holds relationships together. It keeps things steady even when life gets bumpy. Using respectful language is one way to show this. Instead of saying, "That is a dumb idea," try, "I see where you are coming from, but have you thought about this?" Acknowledging what others bring to the table helps everyone feel valued. It is about being a part of a team where every player counts, not just the star.

To make empathy and respect a part of your daily life, try some simple challenges. Pick a day to really listen to someone. Focus on what they are saying without thinking about your reply. Or, practice respectful communication by using kind words even when you are annoyed. These small actions can turn into habits. They help you build stronger, more meaningful relationships. Set goals for yourself, like being more empathetic or catching yourself before you say something disrespectful. Reflect on your progress. Think about how you handled a tricky situation and what you learned. It is all about growing and getting better at this empathy and respect thing.

Kindness Is Key: The Power Of Respectful Engagement

Imagine walking into school when someone holds the door open for you, or maybe you drop your books, and a friend stops to help you pick them up. These small acts of kindness might seem tiny, but they have a big impact.

Kindness is like the secret ingredient that makes relationships respectful and strong. It shows others that you value them and care about their well-being. When you are kind, you create a ripple effect. One kind act can lead to another, spreading positivity like a chain reaction. It is like tossing a pebble into a pond and watching the ripples spread out.

Practicing kindness does not have to be complicated. Start with random acts of kindness. These are small gestures that can brighten someone's day. Compliment a friend on their new haircut or surprise them with their favorite snack. You can also keep a gratitude journal focused on kindness. Write down the kind things you have done and how they made you feel. This exercise helps you see the good in everyday life and motivates you to keep spreading kindness. Incorporating kindness into your routine makes it second nature, like brushing your teeth or tying your shoes.

Kindness impacts more than just individuals. It can strengthen entire communities. When you are kind, you inspire others to be kind, too. And it creates a supportive environment where everyone feels valued. Think about a story where one person's kindness led to a community project or fundraiser. Their actions encouraged others to join in and make a difference.

Kindness builds community bonds and brings people together. It creates a sense of belonging and unity, like a team working towards a common goal.

Cultivating a mindset of kindness starts with mindfulness practices. Focus on compassion by taking a moment each day to reflect on how you can be kind. Think about personal experiences where kindness made a difference. Reflect on those moments and how they felt. These reflections help grow empathy and understanding. They remind you of the power you have to make the world a better place, one simple, kind act at a time.

Healthy Relationships: Setting Boundaries And Expectations

Have you ever felt like you are in a relationship where things just do not feel right? Maybe you were constantly arguing or feeling misunderstood. That is a sign it might not be healthy. A healthy relationship is built on mutual respect and understanding - like a two-way street. Both people listen and care about each other's feelings. Open and honest communication is a must. It is about sharing your thoughts without fear and knowing the other person will listen. When you can talk openly, it makes the bond stronger, and it feels safe and reassuring.

Setting boundaries is also a big part of keeping relationships healthy. Boundaries are like invisible lines that help protect your personal space. They show others what you are comfortable with. It is important to communicate these limits clearly and assertively. If a friend keeps texting late at night and it bothers you, let them know gently. Say, "Hey, I need to sleep at night. Can we chat during the day?" Sometimes, people might cross these boundaries. When that happens, address it calmly. Remind them of your limits. It is not about being mean; it is about taking care of yourself and knowing that upholding your boundaries is important.

Expectations play a huge role in how relationships work. It is important to set realistic ones. If you expect a friend to always be available, you might feel let down. Instead, talk about roles and responsibilities. You may agree to take turns planning hangouts. In partnerships, discuss what each person contributes. Doing this helps avoid misunderstandings and keeps things balanced. It is like being on a team where everyone knows their part. It makes everything run smoother.

Now, conflicts are inevitable, but they do not have to ruin relationships. Resolving them while staying healthy is possible. Practice active listening during disputes.

Really focus on what the other person is saying and avoid interrupting; this shows that you are willing to try and understand. Look for compromise and common ground. Sometimes, both people have valid points. Find a middle ground that works for both. This approach not only solves problems but also strengthens the relationship.

△△△

CHAPTER 11: EMOTIONAL INTELLIGENCE IN THE DIGITAL AGE

"You deserve relationships where you feel valued and respected."

Imagine scrolling through your social media feed. Everyone is posting about their amazing vacations, perfect selfies, and delicious meals. You see all these "perfect" moments and think, "Is everyone living their best life except me?" That is FOMO or the Fear of Missing Out. It is that nagging feeling that you are not part of something awesome. Social media is great for staying in touch, but it can really mess with how you see yourself. It shows idealized images that make you compare your life to others. It is just a highlight reel, not the full movie; you might feel left out, even if your life is pretty great.

FOMO: Navigating Social Media

FOMO is not just about feeling left out, though. It can hit your self-esteem super hard. Seeing everyone's seemingly perfect lives can make you question your own individual worth. You might think you are not doing enough or that you are not good enough. It is important to remember that social media is not the whole picture. People tend to post their best moments, not their struggles. Just like a movie trailer - it is exciting, but it is not the whole story. Real life has ups and downs, and everyone has struggles, even if they do not post them online.

So, how do you handle FOMO and use social media in a healthy way? Start by setting some boundaries. Decide how much time you want to spend scrolling each day; maybe starting with a limit of just an hour or two. Too much time online can affect your mental health. Studies suggest spending more than three hours a day on social media can double the risk of issues like depression and anxiety. So, take breaks and focus on what makes you happy offline. Be mindful of who you follow. Choose accounts that inspire and uplift you. Unfollow or mute those who make you feel bad about yourself.

Building a positive online presence is more than posting perfect pictures. It is about being real and authentic. Share moments that matter to you, even if they are not picture-perfect. It could be a funny meme that made you laugh or a cool hobby you are trying out. Resist the pressure to conform to what everyone else is doing. Be yourself. It is *your* digital space, so make it reflect who you are. Staying authentic can help you connect with others who appreciate the real you. It is like having your very own corner of the internet where you feel comfortable being yourself!

Remember, you are in control of your online experience. You decide what to share and who to engage with. Make it a space that supports your well- being. It is not about likes or followers. It is about expressing yourself and connecting with others in meaningful ways. Social media can be a positive tool if used wisely. But it can be a double-edged sword, cutting you down or lifting you up, depending on how you use it. So, choose wisely and rem- ember that likes and shares do not measure your worth. It is measured by who you are and how you treat others, both online and offline.

Digital Empathy: Kindness In The Online World

Imagine chatting with someone online and not being able to see their face. You cannot tell if they are smiling or frowning. That is where digital empathy comes in. It is different from face-to-face empathy. In person, you can read body language, hear tone, and see facial expressions. Online, you do not have these clues, but empathy still matters. It means understanding and caring about what others feel, even when you cannot actually see them. Digital empathy is about being kind and thoughtful in the virtual world. It is crucial because it helps us connect and support each other, even from miles away.

Practicing digital empathy online starts with your words. Remember, people cannot see your face or hear your voice, so your choice of words is everything. Use considerate language. Instead of saying, "That is a dumb idea," try, "I see your point, but have you thought about this?" It shows respect for the other person's thoughts. Avoid making assumptions about what someone means. If you are unsure, just ask. A quick "Can you explain that more?" can clear up confusion. It also shows that you care to understand. Being thoughtful in your communication can prevent misunderstandings and hurt feelings.

Digital empathy has a powerful impact. It can reduce cyberbullying and create supportive online communities. Imagine a place where people lift each other up instead of tearing each other down. When you show empathy, you set an example. Others might follow your lead. It is like being a light in a dark room. Your kindness can inspire others to be kind, too. And it can change the whole vibe of an online space. Instead of negative comments, you see encouragement and support. Empathy can turn a hostile environment into a welcoming one. It helps build a community where everyone feels safe and valued.

Online interactions might lack the warmth of face-to-face chats, but they do not have to be cold. Empathy can bridge that gap.

It reminds us that there is a person behind every screen, someone with feelings, hopes, and dreams. When we approach online interactions with empathy, we create spaces where people can be themselves without fear. We build connections that are just as real as those in the physical world. Empathy is not just nice to have; it is a way to make the digital world a better place. It is about being there for each other, even when we cannot see each other.

Digital Drama: Handling Online Conflicts

Have you ever been in a group chat where a joke went too far, and suddenly, everyone was upset? Online conflicts happen more often than you would think. It is like trying to read a text message without emojis - you miss the tone, and things get messy. Misunderstandings pop up because you cannot see the other person's face, hear their voice, or see their body language. A sarcastic comment meant to be funny might come off as hurtful. Or a simple question might sound like an accusation. Without context, it is easy for things to spiral out of control. Words on a screen lack the warmth of a face-to-face chat, leaving ample room for misinterpretation.

When online tensions rise, it is tempting to fire back with a quick response. But hold up - take a deep breath and pause! Doing so is your chance to cool down. Then, before you type out that fiery reply, think it through. Ask yourself, "Will this help or just make things worse?" Often, a little time is all you need to see things clearly. If you are still upset, consider addressing the issue privately. A personal message can defuse the situation without an audience fueling the fire. It shows the other person you respect them enough to talk it out away from the crowd. This approach can prevent small misunderstandings from turning into full-blown dramatic events.

Setting boundaries for online communication is not just smart—it is necessary. Think of it as having your own rules for how you interact. Create a personal code of conduct. Decide what topics are off-limits for public discussions. Maybe you prefer not to debate politics or personal matters in group chats. Set limits on when you are available for conversations. It is perfectly okay to say, "I will not respond to messages after 10 PM." This protects your emotional well-being and helps avoid heated late-night exchanges. Boundaries remind you and others that your online space deserves respect, just like your physical space.

Online conflicts can feel overwhelming, especially when they escalate quickly. But remember, you are not alone in this. Many people face digital drama, and it is okay to seek support. Talk to a friend or family member about what is happening. They can offer a fresh perspective or just be there to listen. Sometimes, sharing your feelings can lighten the load. You might even learn new ways to handle conflicts from their experiences. It is important to remember that while online interactions can feel intense, they are just one part of your world. Taking a step back and gaining perspective can help you see the bigger picture.

In the digital age, our screens are windows to so much more than cat videos and memes. They connect us with people near and far, but they can also be breeding grounds for misunderstandings. Handling these conflicts with care can turn a potential mess into a chance for growth. Whether it is taking a pause, setting boundaries, or reaching out for support, you have the tools to navigate digital drama with grace.

Vibing And Thriving: Healthy Digital Habits For Emotional Well-Being

Think of your phone as a sponge, soaking up your time and energy. Sometimes, you need to wring it out and take a break. That is where digital detoxes come in. A digital detox means taking a break from screens to recharge your mind and emotions. Just as one would not run a marathon without rest, you should not scroll endlessly without breaks. When you step away from the digital world, you give your brain a chance to relax. You can go outside, read a book, or just enjoy the quiet. These breaks can help you feel more present and less stressed. It is like hitting the reset button on your brain. You come back to your screens feeling refreshed and ready to think clearly.

When you are online, it is easy to believe everything you see. But not everything is what it seems. Critical thinking is like having a detective kit. It helps you figure out what is real and what is not. Before you share or believe something online, ask yourself a few questions. Who posted it? Why did they post it? Is there proof to back it up? These questions help you see the bigger picture. They stop you from falling for fake news or scams, and you get a better understanding by questioning and exploring. This skill makes you wiser and more informed.

Ghosting is when someone you are talking to online disappears without a word. One moment, you are chatting, and the next moment, they are gone. It can leave you feeling confused and hurt. You wonder why they left and what you did wrong. But often, it has nothing to do with you. People ghost for many reasons, and it is usually about them, not you. If you are the one ending the conversation, try to be respectful. A simple message saying you need some space can go a long way. It gives the other person clarity, even if it is not what they want to hear. This small act, although it may seem difficult, shows kindness and respect for the other person as a human being.

If you have been ghosted, it can feel like a punch to the gut. But there are ways to cope. First, do not blame yourself. Remember, it is usually about them, not you. Talk to a friend or write down your feelings. It helps to get it out. Focus on the people who *are* there for you. Surround yourself with friends who lift you up and make you feel good. Remember, you deserve relationships where you feel valued and respected. Use this experience as a reminder of what you want in your connections with others.

Be Woke: Authenticity And Social Awareness In Digital Spaces

It is easy to feel like you should be someone else online when you have been scrolling and seeing everyone's 'best lives.' But Here is the truth—being yourself is your superpower. Authenticity means being real, even when it is tempting to put on a show. It is about sharing what genuinely interests you, not just what is trending. When you express your true self, you connect with others who appreciate the real you. It is about finding your tribe, the people who get you without any filters. So, how do you stay true to yourself online? Start by posting things that reflect who you are. Share your hobbies, your thoughts, and even those quirky moments.

Building an authentic online presence is about finding balance. It is not just about what you post but how you interact. Engage with others in a way that feels genuine. Comment on posts because you care, not because you feel you have to. Your online persona should reflect your real-life values. If kindness matters to you, let that shine through your interactions. Embrace digital emotional intelligence, understand how your words might impact others, and choose kindness over conflict. This balance creates a positive digital life where you can thrive without the pressure of having to be someone else.

Being socially aware online means looking beyond the screen and seeing the world. It is about sharing information that matters and engaging in causes that you believe in. When you post or share, think about accuracy. Are you helping others by sharing this? Are you supporting a cause that aligns with your values? Social responsibility means using your voice to make a difference, even in small ways. Maybe it is supporting a local charity, sharing a thoughtful article, or simply spreading positivity. Your digital actions can have a big impact, much like ripples in a pond, reaching far beyond what you can see.

To grow in social awareness, follow a range of voices. Listen to people from different backgrounds and experiences, opening your mind to new ideas and perspectives. At the same time, take a moment for self-reflection; ask yourself, "What are my biases?" and "How can I learn from others?" This reflection helps you become more empathetic and understanding. It encourages you to step out of your comfort zone and explore the diverse world around you. Embracing diversity online leads to more meaningful connections and a deeper understanding of the world.

As we wrap up this chapter, remember that your online presence is an extension of who you are. It is a space to be genuine, engage with the world thoughtfully, and grow in understanding. In the next chapter, we will explore how emotional intelligence plays out in the real world, helping you navigate friendships, school, and more.

CHAPTER 12: LIFE SKILLS FOR THE REAL WORLD

Dealing With Disappointment: When Things Do Not Go Your Way

You know that moment when you drop your ice cream cone, and it lands splat on the ground? You watch it melt away and feel that wave of disappointment wash over you. Disappointment can also strike in big ways, like not making the team or getting a lower grade than expected. These setbacks are like little storms that we all face at one time or another. They are a natural part of growing up and learning about life.

Understanding that everyone experiences disappointment can help you feel less alone; you are not the only one who does not understand that tricky math problem. However, life is not about avoiding disappointment - it is about learning how to handle it when it inevitably happens.

Teens face disappointment in many areas. You may not have gotten the part in the play you auditioned for. Your friend forgot to invite you to their party, or that test score was not what you hoped. And boy, do these moments sting. But they also offer a chance to grow. Start by letting yourself feel those emotions. It is okay to be upset. Grab a journal and try to write down how you feel; just let the words flow without judgment. This exercise helps you process your emotions and see them more clearly. Talking to someone you trust can also help. Share your thoughts with a friend, parent, or counselor. They can offer support and a fresh perspective. Remember that it is perfectly okay for you to ask for help when you need it.

Keeping perspective can make a big difference. When disappointment hits, try to look at the bigger picture. Will this matter next week or next month? Practicing gratitude can help you shift your focus. Think about what you are thankful for. Maybe it is your supportive friend or a hobby you love. Reflect on past successes, too. Those moments remind you of your strengths and that setbacks are merely temporary. They are just a small part of your whole story.

Building resilience is like strengthening muscles. The more you face disappointment and bounce back from it, the stronger you become. Think about someone you admire who overcame challenges, such as an athlete who did not win every race but kept on training or an artist who faced rejection but kept on creating. These stories highlight the power of resilience. You can build emotional resilience, too! With each disappointment, there is a chance to learn, adding a new tool to your toolbox. With every challenge, you grow stronger and more prepared for the next one!

Thought Spark: Building Resilience

Think about a time you faced disappointment.

How did you feel?

What did you learn from that experience?

Write down three things you learned about yourself.

How can you use this knowledge to handle future challenges?

Reflecting on these moments helps build your resilience and prepares you for whatever comes next.

The Power Of Persistence: Keep Moving Forward

Picture this: you are trying to learn a new skateboard trick. You fall and scrape your knee, but you get back up. That is persistence. It means sticking with something even when it is hard. It is the key to success. Think about famous folks like J.K. Rowling. She faced countless rejections before Harry Potter became a hit. Or Colonel Sanders, who heard "no" over a thousand times before anyone said "yes" to his chicken recipe. These stories show that success often hides behind challenges, but with persistence, you can push through and reach your goals.

Building persistence is also like building physical endurance - it takes practice. Start by setting small, manageable goals. Let's say you want to run a marathon. You do not start with 26 miles. You begin with just a mile, then two. Be sure to celebrate each milestone, give yourself a pat on the back, or another type of reward along the way that will keep you motivated, such as a favorite snack or a new playlist. These little victories remind you of your progress and keep you moving forward.

Motivation fuels persistence, of which there are two types of motivation: internal and external. Internal motivation comes from within. It is your desire, passion, or love for something. External motivation comes from outside. It might be praise from a teacher or a prize. Find what motivates you! It could be the joy of drawing or the thrill of learning something new. Knowing your motivators helps you keep going, even when things get tough.

Reflecting on past persistence can show you just how far you have come. Think back to a time when you chose to stick with something difficult. Write about it. What did you learn? How did it feel to achieve your goal? Reflecting helps you see your strength and resilience. It is a reminder that you can keep going, no matter what.

Managing Money With Mindfulness

Imagine having a wallet that never seems to stay full. One day, you have the cash to spare, and the next, it is all gone. Learning to manage your money can be tricky at first, but once you get the hang of it, you will be preparing yourself for success. The first step is understanding budgeting. A budget is like a plan for your money. It helps you see where your money goes and how to allocate it better. To start, list your income - things like a steady allowance or part-time job money. Then, write down your expenses - things like clothes, snacks, or movie tickets. When you compare the two, you can see if you are spending more than you earn. It is also important to know the difference between needs and wants. Needs are things like food and school supplies. Wants are extra things, like the latest video game. Knowing this difference helps you make smarter choices.

Mindful spending means thinking before you buy, like taking a moment to decide if you really need that extra-large soda. Keeping a spending diary can help. Write down everything you spend money on for a week. You might be surprised where your money goes. Another tip is the "30-day rule." If you want to buy something big, like a new gadget, wait 30 days. If you still want it after that, go for it. This rule helps you avoid impulse buys and save for what is important.

Setting financial goals helps you plan for the future. You may want to save for a summer trip or college. Start by setting short-term goals, like saving for a concert ticket. Long-term goals could be bigger, like saving for a car. Having goals gives you something to work towards. It makes saving feel less like a chore and more like working towards a dream.

There are tools to make managing money easier. Budgeting apps can track your spending and help you stick to your plan. They show you colorful charts and graphs, making numbers less boring. Teens can also explore bank accounts suited to their needs.

Some accounts come with apps that let you check balances on your phone, making keeping track of your money a breeze. These tools help you stay organized and avoid those "Where did all my money go?" moments.

The Emotion-Logic Tug-Of-War: Finding Balance

Imagine you are trying to decide whether to join a new club or stick with your current activities. Your heart says, "Go for it! It sounds exciting!" But your brain chimes in, "What about your homework and your other commitments?" This is the classic tug-of-war between emotions and logic. Emotions can push us to try new things or take risks. They are the excitement you feel when you see your crush or the fear before a big test. Logic, on the other hand, tells you to think things through. It is the voice that reminds you of your schedule and responsibilities. Your brain processes both, but sometimes they clash, making decisions tough. The key is finding balance and letting both emotion and logic have a say.

Emotional regulation is your secret weapon here. It is about feeling emotions *without* letting them take over. One simple technique is counting to ten before reacting. It gives you a moment to breathe and think.

Reframing your thoughts is another tool. Instead of thinking, "I always mess up," try, "I can learn from this." Acknowledging your emotions is crucial. Do not push them away; instead, say to yourself, "I am feeling nervous," and then work on what to do about it. By recognizing your emotions, you prevent them from controlling your actions. This way, you make decisions with both your heart and your head.

Ultimately, balancing emotions and logic leads to better choices. Imagine a student who balanced both to decide to study abroad. They felt excited about the adventure but logically considered costs and academics. By weighing both sides, they made a choice that felt right. People who have achieved this balance often say it has brought them peace. They feel confident in their decisions, knowing they have considered all aspects.

Finding this harmony means you are less likely to regret your choices, be swayed by every whim, or be stuck in a logical analysis.

Now, let us talk about intuition. Intuition is that gut feeling you get, like an inner compass. It is not the same as an impulse, which is a quick reaction. Intuition is more like a whisper from deep inside. It is based on your past experiences and knowledge. To hone your intuition, pay attention to those gut feelings. Reflect on times when they guided you well. Practice listening to them when making small decisions, like picking a book or choosing a route. Over time, your intuition grows stronger and more reliable.

Thought Sparks: Finding Your Balance

Write down and reflect upon past decisions.

What did emotions say?

What did logic suggest?

How did you balance the two?

Reflecting like this makes you more aware of your decision-making process. It helps you see where you might lean too much on emotions or logic and how to bring both into play.

Thought Sparks: Finding Your Balance

Tap into a decision-making framework. Start with a pros and cons list.

Write down the good and bad for each option, but include how each makes you feel.

Sometimes, seeing it on paper clears the fog.

—

You can use a decision tree, too.

Imagine branching paths for each choice and where they might lead emotionally.

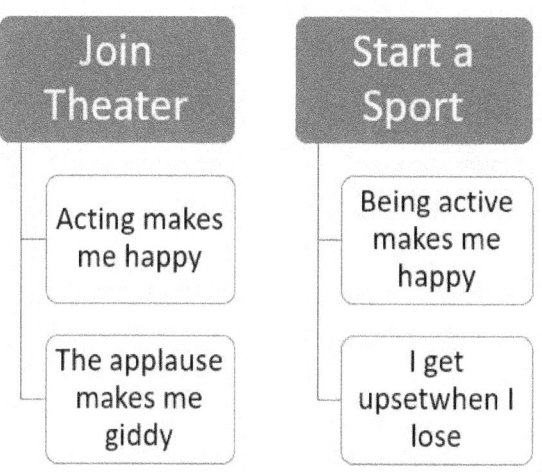

The tree method helps you weigh options with both your heart and head. It lets you see the bigger picture, not just what is right in front of you.

The Calm Mind: Techniques For Clear Thinking

Think of your mind as a busy highway, with cars zooming by at top speed. When you are stressed, it is like a traffic jam in your brain. Your thoughts get tangled, making it hard to think straight. Stress affects your brain's ability to function well. It can make you feel overwhelmed, anxious, and unable to focus. When your mind is calm, you make better decisions. You think clearer, like a smooth road ahead instead of a bumpy one. Staying calm helps you see things as they are, without the fog of stress clouding your judgment.

Mindfulness techniques can help you find that calm. Start with mindful breathing. Find a quiet spot. Close your eyes. Take in a deep breath through your nose, hold it for a moment, and then exhale slowly through your mouth. Repeat this a few times and feel the tension melt away. Guided meditation is another excellent tool. You can find apps or videos that guide you through calming exercises. Visualization is like daydreaming with a purpose. Picture a peaceful place, like a beach or forest. Imagine the sounds, smells, and colors, letting your mind relax. And if an intrusive thought pops into your head - that is OK! Just let it go and continue to melt into the practice at hand. The more you practice this, the fewer intrusive thoughts you will have during these peaceful moments.

Time management is a key component for managing stress. Use a planner or app to keep track of tasks. Break big projects into smaller steps to prevent moments of overwhelm and keep stress in check. Find stress- reducing hobbies such as drawing, gardening, or playing an instrument. These activities give your mind a break, helping you unwind and recharge.

A calming routine sets the tone for your day. Start with a morning ritual, perhaps a few minutes of stretching or sipping tea, and set a calm intention for the day to come.

At night, wind down with a relaxing playlist or a warm bath. Let go of the day's worries.

Creating a calming routine is like setting up a cozy corner for your mind. It gives you a space to breathe and think. With practice, these habits become part of your daily life. They help you stay centered, even when life gets hectic.

Emotional Intelligence In The Workplace: Starting Your Career Right

Starting your first job can feel like stepping into a whole new world. It is exciting and nerve-wracking all at once. Emotional intelligence, or EQ, can make a big difference here. It is not just about doing the tasks. It is about building connections. Much like making friends in school, you will want to build rapport with your colleagues and supervisors. A simple "Good morning" or offering to help can go a long way. When people know they can trust you, it opens doors to collaboration, support, and growth.

Managing stress is another key area where EQ shines. Deadlines, projects, and meetings can pile up fast. It is like juggling; you need to keep them all in the air. EQ helps you stay calm under pressure. Take breaks, breathe, and prioritize your tasks. This way, you can manage your workload without feeling like you are drowning. Sometimes, in a workplace, prioritizing tasks can be difficult, so always be open and willing to ask for guidance.

Understanding workplace dynamics is crucial. Every workplace has its culture, like its own set of unwritten social norms. Take time to observe how people interact. Are meetings formal or more laid-back? Do people like to chat at lunch or keep to themselves? Respecting these norms shows that you are adaptable. Teamwork and collaboration are also vital. Everyone has a role, and working together harmoniously makes things smoother.

For personal growth, seek feedback. Ask your supervisor or coworkers how you are doing and where you can improve. Then, set goals for yourself, both personal and professional. Perhaps you want to learn a new skill or take on more responsibility. These goals give you direction and help you grow in your career.

Real-life examples can inspire you. Take Nancy, an entry-level employee who earned a promotion by honing her communication skills. Nancy sought feedback, learned from it, and then applied it. Or consider Tom, who resolved a workplace conflict using empathy and understanding, turning a tense situation into a positive one. These stories show the power of EQ at work.

CHAPTER 13: THRIVING AND GROWING

YOUR EQ JOURNEY

"Keep a learning mindset is super important. Stay Curious!"

Imagine you are on a camping trip in the woods. It is your first time, and you have no idea how to pitch a tent or start a fire. But you are not worried as you have a trusty guidebook filled with helpful tips and tricks. That is what this chapter is all about—keeping your emotional intelligence sharp, like having a guidebook for life's adventures. Emotional intelligence is like a compass that helps you find your way through tough times. But like any tool, it needs regular updates and practice to stay useful.

Think of emotional intelligence as something that grows with you. It is not just a skill you learn once and forgets about. Life throws all sorts of curveballs at you. As you grow, your emotions change, and so does the way you handle them. Keeping your EQ sharp is about learning every day. It is about being open to new experiences and lessons. You might find that what worked last year does not quite fit this year. That is okay. It is all part of the process.

To keep your EQ on point, try incorporating emotional learning into your daily life. Pick up a book about emotional intelligence. There are tons out there, and some are even written just for teens - like this one! If reading is not your thing, get the book on audio or check out podcasts. Many have episodes about emotional growth that you can listen to while chilling or doing chores.

Workshops and seminars are also great. They often have hands-on activities that make learning fun and interactive. The more you expose yourself to different ideas, the better you will be at understanding and managing emotions.

Feedback is another key player in emotional growth; it acts like a mirror that helps you see things you might miss on your own. Ask friends or mentors for feedback. They can offer insights into how you handle emotions or interact with others. Use this feedback to set new goals.

Perhaps you want to get better at staying calm in stressful situations, or you are working on being more empathetic. Whatever it is, feedback helps you see where you can grow.

Keeping a learning mindset is super important. **Stay curious!** Be open to trying new things, even if they seem a little scary. Identify areas where you want to improve and set a schedule. Maybe you decide to read a chapter of a book each week or join a monthly workshop. Make learning a regular part of your routine. This way, you are always moving forward, keeping your emotional skills sharp and ready for whatever might come next.

Thought Spark: Feedback Reflection

Take a moment to think about a time someone gave you feedback. Jot down what they said and how you felt.

Reflect on what you learned from it.

Did it help you grow or change your approach?

Use this reflection to guide your next steps in emotional learning.

Turning Failure Into Fuel: The Growth Mindset

Imagine you are back on that skateboard, your newest adventure. At first, you fell a lot. But each tumble taught you something new. That was your growth mindset in action. It is about seeing slip-ups as steps forward. A growth mindset means believing you can get better with effort. It is like saying, "I cannot do this... y<u>et</u>." On the flip side, a fixed mindset thinks skills are locked in from birth. If you believe you are just not good at math, that is a fixed mindset talking. But with a growth mindset, you know you can improve with practice and perseverance. This mindset helps you bounce back from those setbacks, prepping you to be ready to try again.

Think of challenges as puzzles just waiting to be solved. Each one is a chance to learn something new. When you hit a roadblock, ask, "What can I learn from this?" Instead of seeing failure as a stop sign, view it as a detour. It could be that you did not make the team this year. That stings, but it is also a chance to train harder and come back stronger. Embrace challenges with curiosity. Step outside your comfort zone. Each new experience is a chance to grow. So, sign up for that painting class. Try out for the upcoming play.

Setting emotional goals gives you direction. These are not just about achieving more. They are about becoming more. With the SMART goal method, your goals become clear and doable. Make them Specific, Measurable, Achievable, Relevant, and Time-bound. Maybe you want to speak up more in class or meetings. Start by setting a goal to raise your hand once a week. Celebrate each small win. Reflect on your progress. Did you speak up? How did it feel? Reflection helps you see how far you have come and where you want to go next.

Feedback is your friend. Ask teachers, mentors, or friends for their thoughts. They can offer a fresh perspective. Use this feedback to tweak your goals.

Let us say that you recently learned that you tend to interrupt others in conversations. Set a new goal to practice listening more. Feedback is not about pointing out flaws. It is about finding new paths to grow.

Igniting *Thought Sparks* and writing them down is a powerful tool for growth. It lets you explore your thoughts and track your progress. Use prompts to get started; there are several throughout this book. Write about a challenge you faced. How did you handle it? What did you learn? Try bullet journaling for a quick, visual way to reflect. Consistent journaling helps you see patterns and celebrate growth. As you look back, you will see how your mindset has evolved. Talk with friends about your mindset shifts. Join a workshop or group discussion. Sharing ideas can spark new insights and reinforce your growth.

Passion Projects: Using EQ To Fuel Your Dreams

Think of your passions as seeds and emotional intelligence is the sunlight that helps them grow. EQ is like a secret ingredient that makes pursuing your dreams not just possible but enjoyable. It boosts creativity, keeps you motivated, and helps you bounce back when things get tough. When you are working on something you love, emotions can run high. EQ helps you channel these feelings into creativity. It turns frustration into fuel and excitement into energy. Think of a musician who uses feelings to create amazing songs or an artist who paints emotions on a canvas. EQ makes these passion projects richer and more meaningful.

Finding the right passion project can sometimes feel like searching for a needle in a haystack. Start by thinking about what makes you happy or what you cannot stop talking about. Have a brainstorming session with friends, and jot down all the ideas that come to mind. Consider what aligns with your values and skills. If you love animals, maybe volunteering at a shelter is your thing. Or, if you are into tech, creating an app might be exciting.

Once you have an idea, set a realistic timeline. Figure out what resources you will need and break it down into steps so it does not feel overwhelming.

Of course, challenges will pop up. That is where EQ really shines. It helps you keep cool and find solutions instead of getting stuck. When obstacles appear, use emotional regulation to stay calm. If a part of your project is not working out, instead of giving up, take a step back and look for another way. Emotional intelligence also means knowing when to ask for help.

Build a support network of friends, family, or mentors who can offer advice and encouragement. Having people in your corner makes a big difference.

Sharing your passion project with others can make it even more rewarding. Look for people who share your interests. Collaborating with like-minded folks can lead to new ideas and different perspectives. Plus, sharing your progress with a supportive community can boost motivation. Whether it is posting updates on social media or joining a club, involving others turns a solo dream into a shared adventure.

The Feedback Loop: Using Constructive Criticism

Imagine you are playing a video game, and you keep losing at the same level. Frustrating, right? Now imagine someone who has already beaten that level offers you some tips. That is exactly what constructive criticism is. It is the feedback that helps you grow and improve, not tear you down. It is important to know the difference. Constructive feedback tells you what you did well and what you can work on, giving you a map to guide you forward. Destructive feedback, on the other hand, just makes you feel bad without helping you improve. In both professional and personal settings, feedback is key. At work, it can help you get better at your job. In your personal life, it can improve your relationships. Listening to feedback helps you see things in a new way, much like wearing glasses that make everything clearer.

Receiving feedback, however, can be tricky. It is easy to feel defensive or upset, but try to see it as a chance to learn. When someone gives you feedback, listen closely. Ask questions if you do not understand something. Doing so shows that you are open to learning and want to improve. It is not about being perfect. It is about getting better. Look at feedback as a tool, not a judgment. It is there to help you, not hurt you.

Giving feedback is just as important as receiving it. When you see someone struggling, your feedback can be the boost that they need. But it is absolutely crucial to do it kindly. Start with something positive, setting a good tone. Then, share what they can work on, but in a helpful way. Try saying, "I liked how you did this, but maybe try this next time." Remember, empathy is a key component here; think about how you would want to hear feedback. This way, you help them grow without making them feel bad.

Feedback loops are powerful. They create a cycle of continuous improvement. Think of a professional ball player who watches game tapes to improve.

They get feedback, make changes, and get better. This leads to success. A personal action plan can help, too. After receiving feedback, jot down what you have learned and your next steps. This practice keeps you focused and motivated. Keep in mind that feedback is not just about fixing mistakes. It is about unlocking your potential. It is about becoming the best version of yourself.

Celebrating Small Wins: Recognizing Progress

Imagine running a marathon. It is not just about the finish line. Every step forward, every mile you conquer, is a victory. In life, small wins are those steps. They build momentum and keep you moving even when the path is tough. Acknowledging these victories is like giving yourself a high-five. It boosts your mood and fuels your drive to keep going. Celebrating small achievements is like feeding your brain a candy bar of happiness. It releases feel-good chemicals, making you more motivated to tackle the next challenge. These little celebrations remind you that you are capable and progressing.

Think of creative ways to celebrate your wins. Create a "win wall" in your room. Fill it with notes or pictures that remind you of each success. It is a visual reminder of what you have accomplished. Or reward yourself with small treats. Maybe it is a special snack, a movie night, or a new book.

These treats do not have to be big. It is about making a moment to recognize your hard work. Sharing your achievements with friends or family can also be rewarding. They can offer cheers and encouragement, making the celebration even sweeter.

Reflection helps you see how far you have come. Set aside time each month to look back on your progress. Think about the goals you have achieved, big or small. What did you learn? What worked well? This reflection helps you appreciate your journey and plan for future growth. You might even keep a journal of these reflections. Write down your thoughts and feelings about each milestone. Sharing these reflections with someone you trust can also bring new insights and ideas.

The power of small wins is huge. They build up over time and lead to big changes. Like drops filling a bucket, each win adds up. It is like climbing a mountain one step at a time.

Before you know it, you are at the top, amazed at how far you have come. Gratitude plays a key role here. Being thankful for what you have achieved fosters a positive mindset. It helps you focus on the good and keep going when things get tough. So celebrate those small wins. They are the building blocks of your success.

Your EI Toolbox: Resources For Continuous Development

Imagine having a toolbox filled with all the gadgets you need to fix any problem. Now, picture a similar toolbox for your emotional intelligence. This EI toolbox is your go-to kit for handling life's emotional ups and downs. It is packed with resources that help you grow, adapt, and thrive. The beauty of an EI toolbox is that it is tailor-made for you. You get to decide what goes in it based on what you need.

Building your toolbox is like curating a playlist for your emotional well-being. Start with books that break down emotional intelligence in a way that resonates with you. There are plenty of titles out there that cater to young adults and teens, offering relatable stories and practical tips. Apps are another great addition. Look for ones focused on mindfulness and emotional tracking. These apps can help you check in with yourself, note your feelings, and even guide you through calming exercises.

An effective toolbox is not static. It needs regular updates to stay fresh and useful. Take time to review what is in your toolbox. It could be that the book you loved last year is not quite hitting the mark anymore. Swap it out for something new. Stay curious about emerging resources. New apps, podcasts, and tools pop up all the time. Trying out different resources helps you find what truly works for you.

Having the right tools can make a world of difference. Investing in your EI toolbox is like investing in your future self. It is about gathering the tools that empower you to handle challenges with grace and strength. As you build and refine your toolbox, you will find yourself more equipped to face whatever comes your way, feeling more balanced and self-assured.

Sample EI Toolbox

James knows that he tends to get easily frustrated when others interrupt him and has been known to blow up when it happens. James started to notice his friendships were suffering, and so he tapped into his EI Toolbox:

> First, he asked for feedback - 'I know that I get upset when I am interrupted - how does it make you feel when I behave this way?' 'Is there a reason for interrupting me?' 'How do you feel I could respond better?'

> He actively listened to his friend's feedback - taking it all in, using thought sparks as a way to reflect on it.

> He advocated for himself by providing constructive feedback to his friends using 'I statements.' - 'When I get interrupted, I feel devalued.' 'It hurts my feelings when I get interrupted; it doesn't feel like people care what I have to say.' 'I would be grateful if you allowed me to complete my sentences.' 'Sometimes I pause to think about my next words, and it is frustrating when I get interrupted during that thought process.'

> He then tapped into mindfulness when he was interrupted, using deep breathing and empathy. Deep breath in, hold it for a beat, slowly breathe out, and think about why they may have interrupted him. Was it relevant to the conversation? Were they just so excited and could not hold it in? Did he pause at a moment when the other person thought he was actually done with his sentence?

> Once calm, he kindly responds to the interruption and redirects the conversation back to what he was saying. 'Ah yes, I understand what you are saying, but to circle back to my original thought...' or 'I hear you! Can we come back to that? I just want to finish out my thought!'

CONCLUSION

As we wrap up our journey together, let us take a moment to remember why we started. This book is all about helping you! Yes, you - become a pro at handling your emotions. Whether it is dealing with stress, making new friends, or figuring out who you really are, emotional intelligence is your secret weapon.

You have gone through chapters packed with skills and insights. First, we tackled self-awareness. Understanding your own emotions is the first step to managing them. Naming your feelings gives you control and clarity. Then, we moved to empathy and how it helps you connect with others. Empathy is not just about feeling for someone else; it is about understanding where they are coming from and feeling *with* them.

Next, we explored social skills. These help you vibe with others, whether you are meeting new people or resolving conflicts in your squad. Emotional regulation has taught you how to keep your cool when emotions run high.

No more outbursts or meltdowns—you have got the tools to stay calm.

We did not stop there. Building self-confidence showed you how to embrace your true self. You learned to celebrate your achievements and strengths. Resilience was another biggie. Life throws curveballs, and bouncing back is key. You discovered how emotional intelligence boosts your resilience.

Ah, and the digital world. Navigating social media and online interactions with emotional intelligence is absolutely vital in today's world. You learned to handle digital drama and maintain your authenticity online.

But here is the thing—emotional growth never stops. It is a lifelong journey. Keep applying what you have learned. Set those personal goals. Practice empathy. Use your Thought Sparks to reflect on your feelings and progress. Emotional intelligence can transform your world. It improves your well-being and strengthens your relationships.

Now, it is your turn to **take action**! Every day is a chance to grow. Make a commitment to yourself to keep on learning. Your journey does not end here. Explore more. Read more. Listen to podcasts. Attend workshops.

Share your journey with others. Build a community of like-minded folks who are also on this path.

As the author, it has been an honor to guide you. I hope this book serves as a trusty friend in your emotional intelligence journey, like having a coach who has got your back.

And always remember, you are not alone. Connect with others who are growing, just like you. Share your victories, big and small. Support each other. Together, you can create a positive and uplifting community.

So here are my final words to you: Believe in yourself! You have got the tools and the power to truly thrive. Emotional intelligence is your ticket to becoming the best version of yourself. So, keep shining bright and go out there with confidence - the world is waiting for the real you!

THOUGHT SPARKS & TECHNIQUES

Throughout this book, we have sparked your thoughts with prompts designed to guide you through journaling your emotions, giving you the keys to unlock 8 Powerful Tools. These tools are your allies in enhancing your people skills, diving deep into personal insights, broadening your social awareness, and mastering everyday stress. We have also shared several techniques to support your journey.

As a special gift, I have gathered all these Thought Sparks and Techniques in one convenient place for you. This collection is your go-to resource as you continue onward on this exciting journey to mastering your emotions!

TOOL #1: Self-Awareness

Thought Spark: Find Your Unique Vibe

- ❖ Write down three things that make you unique.
    - ➤ Are you the one who always knows the best memes?
    - ➤ Do you have a knack for making people laugh?

- ❖ Then, think about why these traits are special.
    - ➤ How do they make you feel?
    - ➤ How do they impact your life?

- ❖ Reflect on how you can embrace these traits even more.

TOOL #1: Self-Awareness

Thought Spark: Finding Your Values

- ❖ Think about moments when you felt truly happy or proud.
  - ➤ What were you doing? Who were you with?

- ❖ Write down a list of different values like honesty, adventure, kindness, or success.

- ❖ Then, rank them by importance.
  - ➤ Which ones feel essential to you?

TOOL #2: Self-Confidence

Thought Spark: Finding Confidence Within

- ❖ Take a few minutes each day to write down three positive things about yourself.
    - ➢ They can be simple, like "I am kind" or "I am creative."

- ❖ Repeat them out loud.
- ❖ Take note of how they make you feel.

TOOL #3: Self-Regulation

Thought Spark: Building Your Self-Control

❖ After a stressful event, take some time to think about it. Write down your thoughts in a journal.

➢ What happened?

➢ How did you react?

➢ What could you do differently next time?

➢ What could you do differently next time?

⋯

TOOL #3: Self-Regulation

Techniques for Keeping Your Cool

- ❖ **3-3-3 Method**
    - ➢ Take a look around you …
    - ➢ Name three things you see;
    - ➢ Focus on three sounds you hear;
    - ➢ And finally, identify three scents around you.

- ❖ **4-7-8 Technique**
    - ➢ Inhale through your nose for four counts,
    - ➢ Hold it in for seven counts,
    - ➢ And exhale slowly through your mouth for eight counts.

- ❖ **Box Breathing**
    - ➢ Inhale, hold, exhale, and hold again.
    - ➢ Each for four counts.
    - ➢ Repeat 4 times

TOOL #4: Empathy

Technique to Improve Empathy & Active Listening

- ❖ Pair up with a friend or family member

    - ➢ One person shares a story, and the other listens <u>without interrupting</u>.

    - ➢ Then switch.

    - ➢ Focus on what the other person says.

    - ➢ Notice their expressions and tone.

    - ➢ Afterward, share what you heard with one another.

TOOL #5: Social Skills

Thought Spark: Vibing with Others

- ❖ Think about how you come across in different social settings.

  - ➢ Are you the center of attention, or do you hang back?

  - ➢ Do you speak up or listen more?

  - ➢ What does your body language look like when you are listening?

  - ➢ What does others' body language look like when you are speaking?

- ❖ Try video recording yourself sometime and look back for things you may not have even realized you were doing.

TOOL #6: Communication

Thought Spark: Discover Your Voice

- Take a few minutes to reflect on your communication style and write down three strengths you have when speaking.

- Then, jot down one area where you would like to improve.

- Consider asking a friend for feedback on how you speak; what do they notice?

- Use this insight to guide your growth as a communicator.

TOOL #6: Communication

Technique for Improving Communication - Mind Mapping

- ❖ Write down your main idea in the center and branch out with supporting points.
    - ➢ This visual guide can help you stay on track during conversations.

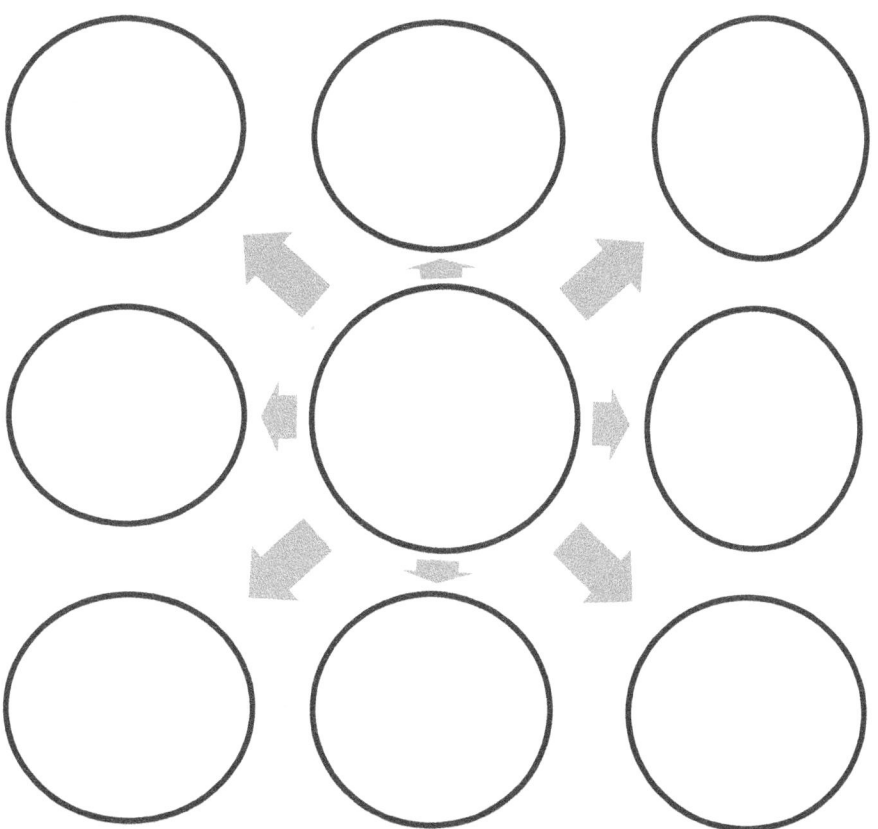

TOOL #7: Motivation

Thought Spark: Discover Your 'Why'

- ❖ Jot down three activities that make you happy.

- ❖ Next, write down why they matter to you.
    - ➢ Look for patterns.

- ❖ What do these activities have in common?

- ❖ Use this reflection to uncover your motivators.

TOOL #7: Motivation

Technique for Setting Goals using S.M.A.R.T.

❖ When setting a goal for yourself, be sure to make it a SMART one! You do that by making the goal:

> ➤ **S**PECIFIC - What exactly do you want to achieve?

> ➤ **M**EASURABLE - How will you know when you have reached it

> ➤ **A**CHIEVABLE - Can you actually do this?

> ➤ **R**ELEVANT - Why does this matter to you?

> ➤ **T**IME-BOUND - When do you want to achieve this by?

For Example: "I want to lose 10 pounds by June 1st by eating healthier and exercising three times a week."

TOOL #7: Motivation

Technique for Staying Motivated using The Pomodoro Technique.

- ❖ Set a timer for a short, focused work session, like 25 minutes, followed by a break.

  - ➢ During those minutes, you work on one task, with no distractions allowed.

  - ➢ When the timer rings, take a short break.

  - ➢ Repeat until the task is complete.

Techniques to Keep the Motivation Alive.

- ❖ Seek out role models or mentors who light that spark.

- ❖ Explore different activities that catch your attention, such as reading biographies of inspiring figures.

- ❖ Enroll in workshops or classes to gain new skills.

TOOL #8: Navigating Change

Thought Spark: Riding the Waves of Change

❖ Take a moment to reflect on a recent change in your life.

➢ What were your initial feelings?

➢ What opportunities did it bring?

❖ Write down how you adapted and what you learned from the experience.

BONUS TOOLS!

Thought Spark: Understanding Your Core Beliefs and Values

❖ Spend some time writing about what truly matters to you.

➢ What are your non-negotiables?

➢ Who do you want to be?

Thought Spark: Building Resilience

❖ Spend some time writing about what truly matters to you.

➢ Think about a time you faced disappointment.

■ How did you feel?

■ What did you learn from that experience?

➢ Now, write down three things you learned about yourself.

■ How can you use this knowledge to handle future challenges?

Thought Sparks: Finding Your Balance Between Emotions and Logic

❖ Write about past decisions.

➢ What did emotions say?

➢ What did logic suggest?

➢ How did you balance the two?

Reflecting like this makes you more aware of your decision-making process and helps you see where you might lean too much on emotions or logic, as well as how to bring both into play.

❖ Try using a decision tree - filling in the branching paths for each choice and where they might lead emotionally.

> ➤ The tree method helps you weigh options with both your heart and head.

Thought Spark: Feedback Reflection

❖ Take a moment to think about a time someone gave you feedback and jot down what they said and how you felt.

➢ Reflect on what you learned from it.

➢ Did it help you grow or change your approach?

❖ Use this reflection to guide your next steps in emotional learning.

Technique to Develop a Personal Code of Ethics

❖ Write down what you believe in and what lines you will not cross.

➢ Keep it somewhere you can see it.

GLOSSARY OF EMOTIONS

Dive into our emotions glossary and spot the feelings that hit home for you. Now, let's boost your emotional vocab! Remember, to master your emotions, you first gotta name them. Each emotion here is unpacked with its definition and a bunch of similar words because, hey, one feeling can wear many hats!

Anger - A strong feeling of displeasure or hostility. *Synonyms: indignation, outrage, rage, fury, wrath, irritation*

Anticipation - The act of looking forward to something with excitement or anxiety. *Synonyms: expectation*

Anxiety - A feeling of worry, nervousness, or unease about an imminent event or something with an uncertain outcome. *Synonyms: fear, worry, concern, unease*

Awe - A feeling of reverential respect mixed with fear or wonder. *Synonyms: amazement, astonishment, admiration, wonderment, wonder*

Compassion - Sympathetic pity and concern for the sufferings or misfortunes of others. *Synonyms: sympathy, empathy*

Confusion - A lack of understanding; uncertainty. *Synonyms: perplexity, bewilderment, befuddlement, bafflement*

Contentment - A state of happiness and satisfaction. *Synonyms: enjoyment, happiness, satisfaction, pleasure, content, delight, joy*

Curiosity - A strong desire to know or learn something. *Synonyms: concern, questioning, inquisitiveness, interest, curiousness*

Disappointment - Sadness or displeasure caused by the non-fulfillment of one's hopes or expectations. *Synonyms: frustration, dismay, dissatisfaction, sadness*

Disgust - A strong feeling of aversion or repulsion. *Synonyms: distaste, hatred, nausea, horror, revulsion, repulsion, disapproval, repugnance*

Embarrassment - A feeling of self-consciousness, shame, or awkwardness. *Synonyms: confusion, humiliation, discomfort, unease, mortification*

Empathy - The ability to understand and share the feelings of another. *Synonyms: compassion, kindness, understanding*

Envy - A feeling of discontent or covetousness with regard to someone else's advantages or possessions. *Synonyms: jealousy, resentment, covetousness*

Euphoric - A feeling or state of intense excitement and happiness. *Synonyms: ecstatic, giddy, elated, excited*

Excitement - A feeling of great enthusiasm and eagerness. *Synonyms: encouragement, stimulation, stimulus, motivation, incentive*

Fear - An unpleasant emotion caused by the belief that someone or something is dangerous. *Synonyms: anxiety, fearfulness, dread, panic, terror*

Frustration - A feeling of being upset or annoyed, especially because of the inability to change or achieve something. *Synonyms: headache, annoyance, nuisance, thorn, worry, exasperation, inconvenience*

Gratitude - A feeling of thankfulness and appreciation. *Synonyms: appreciation, thanks, appreciativeness, thankfulness*

Guilt - A feeling of having done wrong or failed in an obligation. *Synonyms: remorse, regret, shame*

Happiness - A state of well-being and contentment. *Synonyms: joy, bliss*

Hope - A feeling of expectation and desire for a particular thing to happen. *Synonyms: wish, dream, look, purpose, intend*

Hopelessness - A feeling of despair and lack of hope. *Synonyms: desperation, despair, sadness, sorrow, depression, melancholy*

Humble - Having or showing a modest or low estimate of one's own importance. *Synonyms: meek, modest, unassuming, timid*

Humility - A modest or low view of one's own importance; humbleness. *Synonyms: meekness, humbleness, lowliness, modesty, demureness*

Humiliated - A feeling of shame or embarrassment when one's dignity is injured. *Synonyms: embarrassed, disconcerted, discredited, embarrassed, ashamed, humbled, disgraced, degraded, insulted, confused, demeaned*

Inspired - The process of being mentally stimulated to feel or do something, especially something creative. *Synonyms: encouraged, emboldened, heartened, inspirited, stimulated, invigorated, enlivened, elicited, evoked*

Jealousy - A feeling of envy towards someone's achievements or possessions. *Synonyms: resentment, envy, hatred, covetousness, malice, enviousness, animosity*

Loneliness - A feeling of sadness because one has no friends or company. *Synonyms: isolation, solitude, lonesomeness, aloneness, segregation, separateness, seclusion, privacy*

Love - An intense feeling of deep affection. *Synonyms: treasure, appreciate, value, enjoy, cherish, admire*

Nostalgic - A sentimental longing for the past. *Synonyms: wistful, dreamy, sentimental*

Pride - A feeling of deep satisfaction derived from one's own achievements. *Synonyms: pridefulness, confidence, ego, self-respect, dignity, self-regard, assurance*

Regret - A feeling of sadness, repentance, or disappointment over something that has happened or been done. *Synonyms: lament, repent, mourn, rue, deplore*

Relief - A feeling of reassurance and relaxation following the removal of distress or discomfort. *Synonyms: comfort, release, alleviation, ease, consolation, solace, reassurance*

Resentment - Bitter indignation at having been treated unfairly. *Synonyms: offense, huff, frustration, envy, animosity, grudge, grievance, hostility, bitterness, condemnation*

Sadness - The condition or quality of being sorrowful or unhappy. *Synonyms: melancholy, depression, sorrow, grief, mournfulness, anguish, gloom, unhappiness, misery, dejection, despair, oppression*

Shame - A painful feeling of humiliation or distress caused by consciousness of wrong or foolish behavior. *Synonyms: remorse, guilt, regret, remorsefulness, sadness, repentance, disgrace, contempt, humiliation*

Shock - A sudden upsetting or surprising event or experience. *Synonyms: astonishment, amazement, surprise, appall, horrify, stun, scare, frighten, startle*

Surprise - A sudden feeling of astonishment or amazement. *Synonyms: shock, revelation, bombshell, amazement, astonishment, ambush, amaze, shock, stun, startle, astonish*

Suspicion - A feeling or thought that something is possible, likely, or true. *Synonyms: guess, assume, suspect, suppose, think, doubt, skepticism, uncertainty, distrust, mistrust, disbelief, concern, reservation, misgiving*

Trust - A firm belief in the reliability, truth, or ability of someone or something. *Synonyms: believe, accept, take, understand, faith, certainty, credence, assurance*

Vindicated - The feeling of being cleared from blame or suspicion. *Synonyms: exonerated, absolved, confirmed, verified, argued, supported, validated, corroborated, proved, attested*

Yearning - A feeling of intense longing for something. *Synonyms: longing, craving, desire, urge, thirst, hunger*

REFERENCES

- *EQ vs IQ: How They Differ, Which Is More Important?*
  https://www.healthline.com/health/eq-vs-iq
- *8 Activities to Increase Emotional Vocabulary*
  https://www.thoughtco.com/activities-to- increase-emotional-vocabulary-2086623
- Helping your teen navigate their emotional landscape
  https://riseandshine.childrensnational.org/helping-your-teen-navigate-their-emotional-landscape/
- *Emotional Intelligence (for Teens)* https://kidshealth.org/en/teens/eq.html
- *Why Self-Awareness Is Essential for Teenage Students*
  https://www.secondstep.org/blog/self- awareness-is-essential#:~:text=Self%2Dawareness%20functions%20as%20a,feel%E2%80%9D%20amidst%20their%20complex%20experiences.
- *9 stars who have embraced their individuality to the max*
  https://www.bbc.co.uk/programmes/articles/5QWCHVn1XZxMHMVHlH294BK/9-stars- who-have-embraced-their-individuality-to-the-max
- How to Identify and Manage Your Emotional Triggers
  https://www.healthline.com/health/mental-health/emotional-triggers
- *For young adults, mindfulness habits for life and the ...*
  https://www.brown.edu/news/2022-04- 12/mindful-college-student
- Internal vs. External Validation for Self Esteem Growth
  https://foundationsasheville.com/internal-vs-external-validation-for-self-esteem-growth/
- *How Social Media Can Affect Teenage Self-Esteem*
  https://lessonbee.com/blog/how-social- media-can-affect-teenage-self-esteem
- *10 Self-Affirmation Activities to Try* https://psychcentral.com/blog/self-affirmation-a-simple-exercise-that-actually-helps
- *Celebrating Teen Success: The Importance of ...*
  https://drrjjackson.com/celebrating-teen- success-the-importance-of-acknowledging-achievements/
- Mindfulness Exercises (for Teens) | Nemours KidsHealth
  https://kidshealth.org/en/teens/mindful-exercises.html
- *Breathing exercises for stress* https://www.nhs.uk/mental-health/self-help/guides-tools-and- activities/breathing-exercises-for-stress/
- *How to help your teenager manage a meltdown*
  https://www.unicef.org/parenting/mental-health/help-your-teenager-manage-meltdown
- *Promoting Self-Regulation in Adolescents and Young Adults*
  https://fpg.unc.edu/sites/fpg.unc.edu/files/resources/reports-and-policy-briefs/Promoting%20Self-Regulation%20in%20Adolescents%20and%20Young%20Adults.pdf
- *Empathy and Teens: Raising Kids Who Care*
  https://sparkandstitchinstitute.com/empathy-teens/
- *Active Listening Exercises* https://www.centervention.com/active-listening-exercises/

- *How Does Ghosting Affect Teens' Mental Health?* https://bluesprogram.org/how-does- ghosting-affect-teens-mental-health/#:~:text=However%2C%20studies%20actually%20show%20that,frustration%2C%20confusion%2C%20and%20sadness.
- *10 effective questioning techniques | Ideas* https://edu.rsc.org/ideas/10-effective-questioning- techniques/4011025.article
- Social Development | HHS Office of Population Affairs https://opa.hhs.gov/adolescent-health/adolescent-development-explained/social-development
- Empowering Teenager Self-Expression: Embracing ... https://www.jesselebeau.com/empowering-teenager-self-expression embracing-individuality-and-creativity/
- intercultural socialization in adolescents' friendships https://www.sciencedirect.com/science/article/abs/pii/S0147176718304425
- *Cracking the Code: Understanding Body Language in High ...* https://everydayspeech.com/blog-posts/general/cracking-the-code-understanding-body-language-in-high-school/
- *5 Ways to Shake Shyness (for Teens)* https://kidshealth.org/en/teens/shy-tips.html
- *What is the key to open and honest communication ...* https://www.quora.com/What-is-the-key- to-open-and-honest-communication-between-parents-and-teenagers-Why-is-it-important-for-parents-to-remember-this-when-communicating-with-their-teen
- Tips for Teens - Talking to Adults - Centerstone https://centerstone.org/teen/tips-for-teens/
- *Youth Conflict Resolution Techniques + Life Skills* https://elcentronc.org/advocacy/youth- conflict-resolution-techniques-life-skills-processing-conflict-during-a-crisis/
- Motivation and the Power of Not Giving Up (for Teens) https://kidshealth.org/en/teens/motivation.html
- SMART GOALS FOR TEENS - Your Therapy ... https://www.yourtherapysource.com/blog1/2022/08/11/smart-goals-for-teens-3/
- *9 Popular Time Management Techniques and Tools | USAHS* https://www.usa.edu/blog/time- management-techniques/
- 5 TEEN ENTREPRENEURS WHOSE SUCCESS STORIES ... https://www.thestartupsquad.com/5-teen-entrepreneurs-whose-success-stories-wow-and-inspire/
- How to Help Teens Build Emotional Intelligence https://www.newportacademy.com/resources/empowering-teens/teen-emotional-intelligence/
- 5 Strategies to Help Young Adults Navigate Change https://www.newportinstitute.com/resources/mental-health/navigate-through-change/
- *Social and emotional changes: pre-teens and teenagers* https://raisingchildren.net.au/pre- teens/development/social-emotional-development/social-emotional-changes-9-15-years
- How to Help Teens Build Emotional Intelligence https://www.newportacademy.com/resources/empowering-teens/teen-emotional-intelligence/

- *Communication Skills for Teens: 7 Skills Every Teen ...* https://www.daniel-wong.com/2024/04/08/communication-skills-for-teens/
- Conflict Resolution Strategies - 7 Steps To Resolve Teen ... https://paradigmtreatment.com/resolve-a-conflict-7-simple-steps/
- Empathy: How to Feel and Respond to the Emotions of Others https://www.helpguide.org/relationships/communication/empathy#:~:text=Empathy%20allows%20you%20to%20deepen,loneliness%20and%20chat%20with%20them.
- *Social Media and Youth Mental Health* https://www.hhs.gov/surgeongeneral/priorities/youth- mental-health/social-media/index.html
- *Digital empathy* https://en.wikipedia.org/wiki/Digital_empathy
- Using E-Mediation and Online Mediation Techniques for ... https://www.pon.harvard.edu/daily/mediation/dispute-resolution-using-online-mediation/
- *Digital Identity: The Ultimate Guide 2024* https://www.dock.io/post/digital-identity
- *How to Help Teens Deal With Disappointment - Lucero Speaks* https://lucerospeaks.com/how- to-help-teens-deal-with-disappointment/
- 11 Short Stories About Perseverance & Never Giving Up https://www.developgoodhabits.com/perseverance-stories-cm1/
- *Smart Money Management for Young Adults* https://www.fdic.gov/consumer-resource- center/2022-04/smart-money-management-young-adults
- The Importance of Emotional Intelligence in the Workplace https://appliedpsychologydegree.usc.edu/blog/emotional-intelligence-in-the-workplace
- *Always room for growth: Emotional intelligence is a lifelong ...* https://biztimes.com/always- room-for-growth-emotional-intelligence-is-a-lifelong-learning-process/
- *How to Teach Growth Mindset to Teens* https://biglifejournal.com/blogs/blog/teaching-teens-growth-mindset?srsltid=AfmBOorYj-IGZkFTGrKZS7DSukjwabjKTbe5KgYeILisBGl16N7MHrYD
- *Seven Keys to Effective Feedback* https://www.ascd.org/el/articles/seven-keys-to-effective- feedback
- *64 Journaling Prompts for Self-Discovery* https://psychcentral.com/blog/ready-set-journal-64-journaling-prompts-for-self-discovery

"May your emotions be understood, your connections strong, and your resilience unshakable. Welcome to the empowering journey of emotional intelligence!"
-Pearl Fagan

Keeping the Momentum Going

Now that you have the tools to unlock the power of emotional intelligence, it is time to share your journey and help guide others toward their own path of self- awareness and confidence.

By simply leaving your honest opinion of *"The Wonders of Emotional Intelligence for Teens & Young Adults"* on Amazon, you will show parents, educators, and teens where they can find the insights and skills needed to navigate life's challenges with resilience and poise.

Thank you for your help. The world of emotional intelligence grows stronger when we share our knowledge, and you are helping me to do just that!

Scan the QR code to be Directed to the review page on Amazon!

Kindest Regards,
Pearl Fagan

ABOUT THE AUTHOR

Pearl Fagan

Pearl Fagan is an inspiring neurospicy mom of three, celebrated author, wellness advisor, and corporate trainer specializing in emotional intelligence. With decades of experience in mindfulness meditation, a profound understanding of chiropractic care, and a passion for emotional well-being, Pearl empowers individuals to achieve balance and healing in every aspect of their lives.

Pearl's journey into holistic wellness began after an accident that broke her back, leading her to explore chiropractic modalities and mindfulness practices that transformed her recovery and her perspective on health. This life-changing experience inspired her to share these tools with others, leading to a series of books designed to make holistic health accessible and practical for all.

With her warm and engaging writing style, Pearl has become a trusted voice in the wellness community. Her mission is to show that caring for the mind and body is not a luxury but a necessity. Through her books, Pearl has inspired countless readers to embrace practical, evidence-based techniques that fit into even the busiest lives.

BOOKS IN THE WONDERS OF HOLISTIC WELLNESS SERIES

In a world dominated by modern medicine, the timeless wisdom of holistic wellness is more essential than ever. Pearl's series, The Wonders of Holistic Wellness, offers transformative approaches to health and well-being through practical guidance rooted in ancient traditions and modern insights.

From mindfulness meditation to cultivate inner peace and manage stress, to chiropractic care that revitalizes the body and spirit, to the transformative power of emotional intelligence for building stronger relationships and navigating life's challenges, Pearl provides a comprehensive roadmap to total wellness.

Discover actionable steps to reconnect with your mind, body, and soul—empowering you to thrive in every aspect of life.

The Wonders Of Chiropractic: Unbreak Your Back And Revitalize Your Spirit

In this comprehensive guide, Pearl demystifies the world of chiropractic care and empowers readers to make informed decisions about their health. From spinal adjustments to alternative therapies, this book covers all aspects of this holistic approach to well-being.

Learn about the different types of chiropractic treatment and their benefits. Gain valuable insights into choosing the right chiropractor for your needs. And arm yourself with knowledge with a list of questions to ask when contacting a chiropractic office.

The Wonders Of Mindfulness Meditation For Busy Adults: In 7 Easy Steps, Improve Your Mental Health, Achieve Work-Life Harmony, Manage Chronic Pain, And Navigate Everyday Stress

Even if you have never tried meditation before or feel skeptical about visualization techniques, fear not! 'The Wonders of Mindfulness Meditation for Busy Adults' offers a refreshing approach that does not rely on complex visualizations or hours of sitting in silence. Instead, you will discover simple, accessible practices that anyone can integrate seamlessly into their daily routine, regardless of experience level.

With this book as your guide, you will learn how to cultivate mindfulness in a natural and effortless way, allowing you to reap these ancient and incredible benefits without any unnecessary barriers or complications.

Your journey to a happier, healthier, more harmonious life starts right here and now!

BOOKS FROM THE PUBLISHER

At B3H Consulting, Writing, and Publishing, we are passionate about bringing creativity and enjoyment to every generation. In addition to supporting authors on their journeys in both fiction and non-fiction, we craft fun and engaging activity books designed to entertain and challenge children and adults alike.

There is something for everyone! Visit our Amazon store to discover the perfect activity book for your next adventure.

Galactic Freedom: A World UFO Day Activity Book

Galactic Freedom: A World UFO Day Activity Book" is packed with a variety of fun and engaging activities to celebrate World UFO Day on July 2nd.

Inside, you will find crosswords, Sudoku puzzles, word searches, mazes, and coloring pages, all centered around the exciting theme of aliens and UFOs. Each activity is designed to entertain and challenge you while celebrating the inclusivity and wonder of the cosmos.

Get ready to embark on an interstellar adventure and explore the mysteries of the universe with this captivating activity book!

Generation X Activity Book Series

From the Muppets to the A-Team, lose yourself in the nostalgia of the 1970s, 1980s, and 1990s with crossword puzzles, word searches, and coloring pages galore!

Your different books for this series are totally tubular! You can get just one puzzle type in a book! You can get the ultimate 3-in-1 activity book! BEST OF ALL: You have the choice of getting each of these in either a pocket edition or a big print edition! (No cheaters needed!)

www.b3hconsulting.com

www.ingramcontent.com/pod-product-compliance
Lightning Source LLC
Chambersburg PA
CBHW020537030426
42337CB00013B/884